Living and Dying
in Ancient Times

To Joel —

   May the ancestors
be with you.

         Sincerely

DA'AT INSTITUTE
DEATH AWARENESS, ADVOCACY *and* TRAINING

Jewish Life, Death, and Transition Series

Living and Dying
in Ancient Times

Death, Burial, and Mourning
in Biblical Tradition

Simcha Paull Raphael, Ph.D.

Albion
Andalus
Boulder, Colorado
2015

*"The old shall be renewed,
and the new shall be made holy."*
— Rabbi Avraham Yitzhak Kook

Albion-Andalus, Inc.
P. O. Box 19852
Boulder, CO 80308
www.albionandalus.com

Design and layout by Albion-Andalus Books
Cover design by Daryl McCool, D.A.M. Cool Graphics
Cover image: "Rachel's Tomb," wood engraving by John Douglass Woodward, 1881-1884.

ISBN-13: 978-0692495568 (Albion-Andalus Books)
ISBN-10: 0692495568

*This book is dedicated to
Dr. Jean Ouellette
Professor, Études Juives
Université de Montréal –
my first professor of Biblical Studies at
Sir George Williams University
Montreal, Canada
who opened my mind to the world of
Biblical scholarship and study*

Contents

PREFACE

AS A DEATH AWARENESS EDUCATOR, I have spent over three decades teaching individuals and communities about "the mysteries of life, death and the world beyond," particularly as found in both normative and mystical Judaism. Out of a personal and professional conviction to share with others my own understanding of Jewish death traditions, I wrote this book to present a collation of materials on the motifs of death, dying, burial and mourning in Biblical tradition. In particular, this book delineates primarily Biblical narratives chronicling the deaths of our Biblical ancestors, and secondarily subsequent layers of Rabbinic Midrash that attempted to make sense of these Biblical chronicles.

Living and Dying in Ancient Times: Death, Burial, and Mourning in Biblical Tradition is written with a dual perspective—a set of bifocal lenses, if you will—one being *historical,* the other being *contemporary.* On one hand, through the historical lens I explicate views of dying, death, burial and afterlife characteristic of Hebrew and Israelite civilization in the Ancient Near East of the first and second millennia B.C.E., and to a lesser extent of the first millennium C.E.. I illuminate and highlight the rich tapestry of themes found in the Hebrew Biblical tradition, and in so doing, convey a sense of how death was regarded in a world very different from our own.

On the other hand, through the *contemporary* lens I strive to extract from the rich tapestry of Biblical and Rabbinic texts contemporary reflections on dealing with death and dying in our ever-changing twenty-first century society.

I do believe that both Torah—reflecting the *ancient Israelite past*—and Midrash—reflecting *generations of post-Biblical Rabbis* who told and re-told tales from Torah—have a great deal to offer our contemporary society. In this era of highly technological deathbed experiences, we desperately need healthy, ideal models for learning how to respond to death, dying, burial and mourning with a sense of spiritual understanding. In writing this book, my underlying motivation at all times has been to harvest from Jewish tradition philosophical wisdom and practical guidelines for dealing with all facets of the human encounter with death in our post-millennial age of transition and transformation.

This book is part of the Albion-Andalus *Jewish Life, Death and Transition* series. I wish to thank

Netanel Miles-Yépez for his vision to create this series, and for his editorial acumen that helped shape this book.

I also wish to thank Rabbi Michael Pitkowsky and Rabbi Jill Hammer of the Academy for Jewish Religion who supervised my original research on this topic; David Zinner, of Kavod v'Nichum and Dr. Jean Ouellette, both of whom offered editorial input; Dr. Shaul Magid who authored the Foreword to this book, and to my teacher and mentor, Rabbi Zalman Schachter-Shalomi, of Blessed Memory, who inspired my work in the area of Jewish perspectives on death and the afterlife.

I also offer deep-felt appreciation and thanks to my wife, Rabbi Geela Rayzel Raphael. She has been my life companion for over three decades, a loyal partner and co-parent, who is a passionate ally and source of support in all my artistic, creative and intellectual endeavors.

Finally, I am ever-grateful for the opportunity to share the fruits of my own learning with others, and thank the Holy One of Blessing who has given us life and vitality, sustained us, and brought us to this moment.

— SIMCHA PAULL RAPHAEL
Melrose Park, PA
July 1st, 2015
14 Tammuz 5775

FOREWORD

THERE IS A RABBINIC MIDRASH that teaches: Adam and Eve were created in the afternoon on the sixth day of creation. As the sun began to set and dusk descended, they thought this was the end of creation and thus their deaths. They found a rock where they watched the sun set, and as darkness fell, they cried all night waiting for their end. In the morning, as the first rays of sun appeared, they realized they were still alive. They sang, "Sing a song of *Shabbat*. It is good to thank God and to give praise to God's holy name."

Like all religious traditions since the advent of humankind, Judaism is both enraptured by, and in fear of, death. Some traditions have well-known books of the dead, e.g. the Tibetan Book of the Dead, the Egyptian Book of the Dead. Judaism does have a correlate book of the dead—*Maavor Yabok,* authored by Rabbi Aaron Berechiah of 17th century Mantua, Italy. But it is largely unknown to contemporary Judaism. But in the Hebrew Bible and subsequent Rabbinic literature, death, the very cessation of life as well as ruminations of the afterlife, play a major role.

How biblical figures die, when they die, where they die all were of paramount importance for Israelite and later Jewish writers. There are long descriptions of buying burial chambers (e.g. Abraham buying the Cave of Machpelah for his wife Sarah) and last wills and testaments (e.g. Jacob's blessing to his children before his death at the end of Genesis). In some way, the second half of Deuteronomy is all about Moses' imminent passing, preparing his community for his absence. There are those, such as Moses and his brother Aaron, who die with a kiss, others like Korach who are swallowed up by the earth, and still others such as Enoch and Elijah, who do not really die at all but experience a kind of apotheosis and their spirits hover over the world to this day. Moses views it as a tremendous responsibility to carry Joseph's bones out of Egypt to bury him in the Land of Israel. And the matriarch Rachel dying "on the way" results in her burial place becoming a monument and a symbol for Israelite exile. So while Jews generally do not appear to have a Book of the Dead like ancient Egyptians or Tibetans, Hebrew Scripture and its interpreters are certainly deeply concerned about death and all that follows; burial, mourning, and the barriers that separate the dead from the living.

There are extended Talmudic dicta on the

laws of mourning *(aninut* and *avelut)* and traditionally students studying for the rabbinate had to master these laws as a pre-requisite for ordination. Customs like sitting *Shiva,* a seven-day mourning period, reciting the Kaddish prayer, recited by blood relatives after the passing of a loved one, are some of the practiced customs in Judaism, even for those who have abandoned almost everything else. The French film, *The Jewish Cardinal,* about the life of the Jewish convert Cardinal Lustiger of France is centered around his not saying Kaddish for his father and his last request that Kaddish be said at his funeral (it was). Collective customs of mourning—not getting married on the forty-nine days between Passover and Shavuot because it was a time the students of Rabbi Akiva, the great rabbinic sage, had died in a plague, and enacting rites of collective mourning to commemorate the destruction of the Jerusalem Temple on the 9th day of the Hebrew month of Av—are an integral part of the warp and woof of Jewish ritual and liturgical life.

Judaism is a religion that values life, but it is also very taken up with death and its implications. How the soul leaves the body, its transitional period for the first year in a state of perpetual judgment and cleansing, and its final resting place thereafter is a major topic in Jewish scholarship. Kabbalists argue that the line separating the living from the dead is less opaque than we think and communication between departed souls and living beings is possible. Soul impregnation, that is, the souls of departed ones entering into living bodies, and reincarnation, are not ideas foreign to Judaism.

In *Living and Dying in Ancient Times,* Simcha Raphael gives us a wonderful and thorough introduction to the various ways ancient Israelites understood death and dying, its implications and its effect on the living. As is true in many ancient languages, important concepts have multiple words to describe it. This is certainly the case with "death" in the Hebrew Scriptures. Who dies, how they die and how to die are all of concern. Death in Judaism is viewed in some ways as the very epitome of life. And as expressed in the Rabbinic *midrash* about Adam and Eve, death remains the most horrifying and unknowable, yet inevitable, of human experiences. Like many other traditions, Jewish reflection on death and dying inhabits the space between these two expressions: death as that which we all prepare for, and death as that which we are all unprepared for. Simcha Raphael's book is a welcome study of the myriad ways this unavoidable and yet anxiety-producing moment is treated in ancient Jewish sources. *Living and Dying in Ancient Times* does not offer any answers to the perennial question, "what happens when we die?" but it does open vistas for further exploration into the ways death and dying informs the Jewish tradition, the lives of its mythic personalities, as well as anyone who feels connected to that tradition, or any tradition, on these questions.

Adam and Eve realized from experience that sunset did not mark the end of creation and therefore their deaths. But they also learned from experience that everyone, including themselves, one day will die. This is our inheritance, to be blessed with life and bequeathed death. To know both, even if we don't understand either, is to be able to live fully in this beautiful creation we call our world.

— SHAUL MAGID, PH.D.,
Bloomington, IN
Jay and Jeannie Schottenstein Professor
of Jewish Studies, Indiana University

Living and Dying
in Ancient Times

Death, Burial, and Mourning
in Biblical Tradition

the bereaved to mourn and experience the multi-dimensional nature of grief.

Yet within our contemporary Western cultural context, there is often a tendency to deny and sanitize the reality of death and grief. In general, there is an uncomfortable reticence to speak openly about it. People do not die, they "pass" or "expire." Bereaved are discouraged from mourning, told not to cry. Children are all-too-often shielded from the reality of death. And our elders are confined to "nursing homes" where little is spoken of the omnipresence of both death and grief, as if denying death can keep away its inevitability.

This attitude, characteristic of modern Western culture, stands in sharp contrast to ways in which Judaism and Jewish tradition have traditionally responded to death. Long before the seemingly ubiquitous influence of a worldview of secular, scientific materialism, Judaism developed a philosophy of life and death that accepted death with a realistic openness. Over the course of millennia, Jewish culture spawned an integrated system of ritual practices providing emotional comfort, communal support and spiritual solace in times of death and loss. In contrast to Western culture of the second half of the twentieth century and to present times, Judaism has a healthy approach to death, burial and mourning, seeing death as inherently part of life in both philosophical orientation and through a well-defined set of ritual practices.

As an antidote to the death-denying view of Western culture, we need healthy and creative approaches to the reality of death and loss today. I believe we can find a great deal of applicable contemporary wisdom on death in the teachings, tales and traditions of the Hebrew Bible. In this book, I present a collage, a pastiche of images and motifs on death, dying, burial and mourning in Biblical tradition and Rabbinic Midrash.

The outline of the remainder of this book is as follows:

"A Lexicon of Biblical Terms for Death and Dying" delineates the philosophy of life and death portrayed in various terms related to death found in the Hebrew Bible.

"Images and Motifs of Burial" explores varied depictions of the funeral and burial experiences of our Biblical ancestors Sarah, Rachel, Jacob and Joseph. This chapter reveals a tapestry of approaches to death and burial very different than what we find in contemporary culture. It certainly raises the question as to what are "normative" or "traditional" forms of burial.

"Mourning in Bible and Midrash" examines different images of mourning practices in Biblical and Rabbinic texts. From this chapter, we see both Ancient Near Eastern mourning practices radically different than our own, and early antecedents and textual traditions that form the basis for the development of Jewish mourning rituals.

"Moses' Death and the Stages of Dying" looks at a unique compilation of Biblical and Rabbinic texts through the lens of Elisabeth Kübler-Ross' stages of dying.[1] In exploring a little-known set of Jewish legendary materials, we see ways of making traditional material relevant for a contemporary approach to hospice and care for the dying.

Finally, "Envisioning a Renewed Philosophy of Death" concludes this study with reflections on contemporary implications of Biblical ideas of death, burial and mourning.

In no way can this book seen as a complete study of the topic of death and mourning in Biblical tradition. The scholarship of Rachel S. Hallote,[2] Philip S. Johnston,[3] Saul M. Olyan,[4] Xuan Huong Thi Pham[5] and Nicholas J. Tromp[6] addressed this topic with far more depth. However, consistent with the objectives of the "Jewish Life, Death and Transition Series," the goal in writing has been to present a portrayal of Biblical ideas of death and mourning for those who are seeking contemporary wisdom on the human encounter with death.

A Lexicon of Biblical Terms for Death and Dying

As a way to depict central attitudes and ideas toward death characteristic of ancient Biblical times this chapter presents a lexicon of various terms for death in the Hebrew Bible.[7]

In modern Hebrew, the term for death is *mavet*, and the word for a dead body is *met*. However, in ancient Biblical tradition, death is described in a wide variety of different ways. Words for death, which translate as "expired," "slept with his ancestors," or "gathered to his people"— among others—all allude to a complex worldview regarding life, death and the world beyond. The various terms used to refer to death and dying in Biblical tradition portray a richly-textured, fascinating understanding of death, and a radically different philosophy of life than what we often take to be normative in Western culture.

Mavet — Death

First and foremost, the term *mavet* is used to describe death. But generally it is used quite simply and prosaically. Speaking of the death of Sarah, Gen. 23:2 states: *va'tamat Sarah*, "And Sarah died."

In Gen. 20:3, when God appears to Abimelech in a dream, telling him he will die, the text reads: *hineha met*—"you are to die" ("you are but a dead man" according to another translation). Similarly, in Num. 20:1, when the Israelites came "into the desert of Zin in the first month; and the people abode in Kadesh …" the text states quite simply, with no fanfare or ritual elaboration—*va'tamat sham Miriam*—"and Miriam died there."

In a similar mode, in Gen. 35:8 we read about a little-known, enigmatic woman named Deborah who served as Rebecca's wet-nurse. Again, without fanfare or drama, the text speaks of her death: "And Deborah, Rebecca's nurse, died, and she was buried under the oak below Bethel"—*"va'tamat Devorah Mineket Rivkah, va'tikaver mitahat l'veit El, tahat ha'alon …"*

It is interesting that these three examples in which the word *mavet* appears, describe the deaths of women, and their deaths are noted with no elaboration or description, nor any deathbed reflections or last words. Even more, the death of Isaac's wife Rebecca and Jacob's first wife Leah are not even mentioned at all in the Bible. By way of contrast, the deathbed scenes of both Jacob and Joseph are far more elaborate, with time allotted for reflection and last wishes. And, as we shall see below, the phrase used for death when Abraham, Isaac and Jacob die is being "gathered to one's ancestors."

So the term *mavet* connotes the end of life on the physical plane, and it appears there are no other obvious associations.

Va'yigvah — Expired

Translated as "expired," "perished," or "died," the term *va'yigvah* first appears in Gen. 7:21. Describing collateral damage from the climate change weather catastrophe we have come to call "The Flood," the Torah says: "And all flesh died that moved upon the earth, both of bird, and of cattle, and of beast, and of every creeping thing that creeps upon the earth, and all humankind." The term for died in this sentence—*va'yigvah*—is clearly connoting loss of life. The following verse (Gen. 7:22) clarifies this further: "All in whose nostrils was the breath of life ... died." Implied here is the notion of life itself being synonymous with breath: in creating human life, in creating the first person, Adam, God "breathed into this nostrils the breathe of life" (Gen. 2:7)—*va'yippakh b'apav nishmat ḥayyim*. And, as a corollary, the removal of breath is termination of life, death—*va'yigvah*.

This term *va'yigvah* is used in many Biblical death narratives. "Abraham expired—*va'yigvah*—and died in a good old age ..." (Gen. 25:8) "Isaac expired—*va'yigvah*—and died ... being old and full of days." Gen. 35:29) "Jacob finished commanding his sons, gathered up his feet into the bed, and expired—*va'yigvah.*" (Gen. 49:33)

Of Aaron's death, Torah states:

> Moses stripped Aaron of his garments, and put them upon Eleazar his son; and Aaron died there in the top of the mount ... And when all the congregation saw that Aaron was dead (i.e. had breathed his last)—*ki gavah Aharon* [a variant verb form, but still meaning expired]—they mourned for Aaron thirty days. (Num. 20:28-29)

Going one step further: *va'yigvah* is related etymologically to the Hebrew word—*geviah* (Nah. 3:3)—a corpse or dead body. *Geviah* is a devitalized physical body, a de-animated human being whose breath has been fully taken away. Thus, in the early Biblical world, death is not, as we have it today, an annihilation of existence caused by the cessation of brain function and heartbeat. Nor do we find in the early Biblical worldview a conception of death as the separation of body and soul. This idea of body-soul dualism is a much later development that emerges for the first time in the Graeco-Roman period.[8] Instead, the term *va'yigvah* implies that death is regarded as a progressive diminution of energy and vitality, of life force and breath.

Life and death are complementary poles of a

continuum of vital energy. In creating humanity, God breathed the breath of life—*nishmat ḥayyim*—into Adam, and Adam became *nephesh ḥayyah* (Gen. 2:7), a living *nephesh*, a living spirit— an alive human being, a vitalized psycho-physical entity. Sickness is a slow dissipation of that energy and vitality, an energetic wasting-away. And at the other end of the continuum, death is the final and total diminution of breath, life force and vitality. In death, with the final dissipation of breath and life force, one becomes *nephesh met* (Lev. 21:11; Num. 6:6), a dead *nephesh*, a de-potentiated psycho-physical entity.

Thus the notion of death encoded in this term *va'yigvah* tells us that our Biblical ancestors understood death, not as a single event, but as a process involving the progressive transformation, diminution and depletion of psychic energy.

Va'yeasef el Amav —
Gathered to His People

The term *va'yeasef el amav*—"was gathered to his people"—is found quite frequently in the Torah. In Genesis, this phrase occurs consistently in describing the deaths of the Patriarchs. Thus, we see Abraham, "died in a good old age … and was gathered to his people"—*va'yeasef el amav* (Gen. 25:8); Isaac "expired, and died, and was gathered to his people"—*va'yeasef el amav* (Gen. 35:9); and Jacob "finished commanding his sons, gathered up his feet into the bed, and expired, and was gathered to his people"—*va'yeasef el amav* (Gen. 49:33).

In these various passages, death is described not just once, but in two or sometimes three different ways: Abraham "died in a good age;" Isaac "expired;" and Jacob "gathered his feet into the bed and expired." But along with those specific terms, it is said of each of them, "he was gathered to his people".

What exactly does it mean to be gathered to one's people? Is this notion to be understood literally? Or as metaphor and symbol? And if the latter, symbolic of what?

We know, at least according to Biblical tradition, that Abraham, Isaac and Jacob are buried in the same family sepulcher in Machpelah. As we explore below, a great deal of attention and intention was focused on the desire of the later Patriarchs to be returned to Machpelah for burial. Where they are interred—"in the cave in the field of Ephron the Hittite, at Machpelah" (Gen. 49:29-30)—is not simply a matter of convenience or happenstance. Each time the Patriarchs speak of their intended place of burial, it is clear they are very intentional and determined in requesting internment at Machpelah with their ancestors. The idea of burial in collective family tombs or caves was central to ancient Israelite burial practices. It was common for the deceased to be placed in hewn cave tombs or sepulchers which housed many different deceased family generations.[9]

Is the phrase describing death as being "gathered to one's people" merely a reiteration of the obvious, indicating that they are now to be buried in the same family tomb with their deceased relatives? Reading the narrative description of Joseph's death and burial could lead to this conclusion. Found at the end of Genesis, the text describing Joseph's death is categorically different than that of his deceased ancestors: "Joseph died, being a hundred and ten years old; and they embalmed him,[10] and he was put in a coffin in Egypt." (Gen. 50:26) In this passage, there is absolutely no mention of Joseph being "gathered to his people." Unlike his father Jacob, grandparents Isaac and Rebecca, and great-grandparents Abraham and Sarah before him, Joseph is not buried at Machpelah. He is entombed in Egypt, and only later is he brought into the Land of Israel in the time of Joshua; but he is not buried at Machpelah. So does the idea of being buried in the family tomb really explain use of the phrase "gathered to his people"?

The answer to this question is not so simple. In the deathbed accounts of Aaron and Moses, we do again find that familiar phrase "gathered to his people." Deut. 32:48-50 presents a very clear death proclamation from God to Moses, saying:

> Go up to this Mountain Abarim, to Mount
> Nebo, which is in the land of Moab, that is
> opposite Jericho; and behold the land of
> Canaan, which I give to the people of Israel
> for a possession; And die in the mount where
> you go up, and *be gathered to your people*; as
> Aaron your brother died in Mount Hor, and
> *was gathered to his people.*

Both Aaron and Moses are said to be gathered to their people, but neither of them are buried in a family tomb. If anything, it is just the opposite: the two brothers each have a solitary desert burial, Aaron atop Mount Hor (Num. 20:25-29), and Moses "in a valley in the land of Moab, opposite Beth-Peor; [where] no man knows his grave till this day." (Deut. 34:6) So perhaps the idea of "gathered to his people" has a different connotation, referring to something more than localized burial in a family tomb.

In an article entitled "Death in the Bible," Jacob Chinitz suggests that perhaps the metaphor of being gathered to his people is "used to convey the idea of entering a spiritual realm of his people, regardless of the actual place of burial."[11] Thus, the author continues, "the idea of a spiritual ingathering becomes imperative."[12] Perhaps this phrase "gathered to his people" alludes to the idea that the death experience is some type of postmortem ingathering, a welcoming of those who have recently died by previously deceased family. This idea is certainly consistent with the findings of contemporary near-death experience literature that speaks of how at the time of death one has visions of deceased relatives.[13] Even more specifically, although from an era almost two millennia later, we find in the Zohar—a mystical commentary on the Torah—numerous statements such as this:

> Rabbi Shimon said: Have you seen today the image of your father? For so we have learnt, that at the hour of a person's departure from the world, one's father and one's relatives gather round, and one sees them and recognizes them, and likewise all with whom one associated in this world, and they accompany one's soul to the place where it is to abide. (Zohar I, 218a)

It is hard to know for sure that this phenomenon of encountering deceased family members is what the Biblical authors were speaking of in writing about how Abraham, Isaac, Jacob, Aaron and Moses were "gathered to their people". But it certainly suggests that the Torah is alluding to the notion that there is but a translucent screen between this world and the world beyond, traversed at the time of one's death. And upon entering that world beyond, there are deceased family members to welcome one who has just died.[14]

Va'yishkav im avotav —
He Slept with His Ancestors

Another phrase found in the Hebrew Bible describing death is *va'yishkav im avotav*—"and he slept with his ancestors." This has connotations similar to "he was gathered to his people"—*va'yeasef el amav.* At times, the two terms may be used interchangeably. For example, in Deut. 31:16, being informed of his pending death, Moses is told by God: "Behold you are going to lie [sleep] with your ancestors [fathers] ..." But in the next chapter, again Moses is told by God he shall die—and the phrase here for death is "will be gathered to your people." (Deut. 32:50)

It would appear these two terms are parallel expressions. Certainly the traditional Biblical commentators, Radak (on 2 Kings 24:6) and Ibn Ezra (on Dan. 1:1) assumed that these two terms "gathered to his people" and "slept with his ancestors" are synonymous.[15]

Shaul Bar, author of *I Deal Death and Give Life —Biblical Perspectives on Death* notes the phrase "he was gathered to his people" appears frequently in the Torah, whereas "he slept with his ancestors" is found in *Nevi'im* (Prophets) and *Ketubim* (Writings).[16] For example, of King David

it is written: "David slept with his ancestors—
va'yishkav im avotav—and was buried in the city
of David." (1 Kings 2:10) Similarly, it is said of King
Solomon—"Solomon slept with his ancestors—
va'yishkav im avotav - and was buried in the city
of David his father." (1 Kings 11:43) (See also Judg.
2:10; 2 Kings 22:20; 2 Chron. 34:28).

According to Bar, both "these expressions stem
from the idea that a person is buried in the family
tomb where he joins his ancestors who pre-
deceased him."[17] And while (as we noted above)
the notion of literally returning to the family tomb
for burial does not apply when used with Aaron
and Moses, there is no doubt that the practice
of burial in family tombs was central to ancient
Israelite burial traditions.

Extrapolating from the foregoing, we can
conjecture that both phrases "he was gathered
to his people" and "he slept with his ancestors"
suggest that upon death there was a sense of re-
connection and continuity with the tribal family
in a mysterious yet palpable postmortem realm.

B'tzait naphsha — As Her Soul Was Departing

One additional term in the Hebrew Bible
referring to death is *b'tzait naphsha*—"as her soul
was departing." This phrase appears only once,

and is used in describing the death of Rachel in childbirth.

According to Gen. 35:17-19:

> And it came to pass, when she was in difficult labor, that the midwife said to her, "Fear not; you shall have this son also." And it came to pass, as her soul was departing—*b'tzait naphsha*—for she died, that she called his name Benoni; but his father called him Benjamin. And Rachel died, and was buried in the way to Ephrath, which is Beth-Lehem.

In recounting Rachel's death, the text never states she is gathered to her people, nor does she sleep with her ancestors. Of all the Patriarchs and Matriarchs, it is Rachel alone who is not buried in the family tomb at Machpelah. Interestingly, here the fact of death is viewed as a durative process, not a single, momentary event. Essential to this process is the progressive departure from the body of an entity called *nephesh*—best understood as spirit or life force. No one else's death in all of Biblical tradition is delineated with this particular term. Perhaps this particularly poignant and unique image is used to highlight the reality of Rachel's death as a holy and beloved wife and mother who has suffered through a difficult and fatal childbirth.

Notwithstanding, what is revealed here is the

sense of dying as a transitional process of the life force leaving the body. What a simple and yet profound realization bequeathed to our age by the authors of the Bible.

IMAGES AND MOTIFS OF BURIAL

Sarah's Death
and the Cave at Machpelah

GENESIS CHAPTER 23 PRESENTS the first and most elaborate description of the purchase of a burial plot found in the Hebrew Bible. The chapter begins with news of Sarah's death in "*Kiriath-Arba*; which is Hebron in the land of Canaan" at 127 years of age. The text then tells us that "Abraham came to mourn for Sarah, and to weep for her." (Gen. 23:2) What follows in the remainder of the chapter is a description of Abraham's focused effort to purchase land for Sarah's burial. We read about his deliberations with the Hittites requesting of them to:

> ... entreat for me to Ephron the son of Zohar. That he may give me the cave of Machpelah, which he has, which is in the end of his field; for as much money as it is worth he shall give it me as a possession of a burying place amongst you. (Gen. 23:8-9)

The recently bereaved Abraham and Ephron the Hittite enter into financial negotiations with Abraham weighing out four hundred shekels of silver in return for a burial plot for his deceased wife Sarah. The result, an honorable resting place for Sarah, and a burial site which forever remains a noted location in Jewish history and experience:

> And the field of Ephron, which was in Machpelah, which was before Mamre, the field, and the cave which was in it, and all the trees that were in the field, that were in all the borders around, were made over to Abraham for a possession in the presence of the Hittites, before all who went in at the gate of his city. And after this, Abraham buried Sarah his wife in the cave of the field of Machpelah before Mamre; the same is Hebron in the land of Canaan. And the field, and the cave that is in it, were made over to Abraham for a possession of a burying place by the Hittites. (Gen. 23:17-20)

An imperative for burial in the Cave of Machpelah remains central throughout subsequent death narratives in Genesis. At the time of Abraham's death, described as being "gathered to his people," we are once again reminded of Abraham's initial purchase of Machpelah, and informed that:

> ... his sons Isaac and Ishmael buried him in the cave of Machpelah, in the field of Ephron the son of Zohar the Hittite, which is before Mamre; the field which Abraham purchased from the Hittites; there was Abraham buried, and Sarah his wife. (Gen. 25:9-10)

When Isaac dies, he is living at Hebron, and although the text does not specifically say where he is buried, we can assume it is at Machpelah where "his sons Esau and Jacob buried him." (Gen. 35:29)

Before Jacob dies, he gathers together his children, and as part of his end-of-life closure reiterates for them the history of the purchase of the Cave of Machpelah:

> And he charged them, and said to them, I am to be gathered to my people; bury me with my fathers in the cave that is in the field of Ephron the Hittite, in the cave that is in the field of Machpelah, which is before Mamre, in the land of Canaan, which Abraham bought with the field of Ephron the Hittite for a possession of a burying place. There they buried Abraham and Sarah his wife; there they buried Isaac and Rebecca his wife; and there I buried Leah. The purchase of the field and of the cave that is in it was from the Hittites. (Gen. 49:29-32)

We can imagine the scene here of Jacob, surrounded by members of his family-clan—children, grandchildren, great-grandchildren, and daughters-in-law—all present, paying attention to the final words of the dying old man. Fully lucid and with deliberate clarity, Jacob asserts the importance of his being buried in the ancestral family tomb at Machpelah, and names specifically all of his ancestors already buried there.

We glean from Jacob's words of farewell that he is saying much more than: "Children, please note, this is where I own a burial plot!" We know decent burial was of great importance in the Ancient Near East and Mesopotamia, with people dreading the thought of lying unburied in the harsh desert sun. But in the above passage from the final chapters of Genesis, Jacob's parting words to his family are not only a functional request, but also a spiritual one. For Jacob, burial at Machpelah, in essence, meant entering the ancestral realm of the family tomb upon departing this world. As noted in the previous chapter, in being "gathered to his people," one would be reunited with previously deceased ancestral family members.

Over and over, in Torah and later Biblical writings, great importance is placed upon being buried along with one's family members. All of Jacob's ancestors, as well as his first wife Leah were buried in the family tomb at Machpelah.[18] Similarly, King David was laid to rest in the Citadel of David, a family tomb (1 Kings 2:10) and the Book of Kings documents how the later Kings of Judah were buried with their ancestors, in the Davidic family tomb,[19] including Rehoboam (14:31); Asa (15:24); Jehoshaphat (22:51); Uzziah (2 Kings 15:7); Jotham (15:38); and Ahaz (16:20). Saul, the first King of Israel, and his son Jonathan were buried in the tomb of Saul's father, Kish. (2 Sam. 21:1-14)

As an Ancient Near Eastern civilization, Biblical Judaism was tribal in nature, and the central social organism was the family clan. Like the wandering Bedouins of today, the early Hebrews traversed the ancient deserts in large extended families—men, women and children; sheep, goats and camels— living, working and worshipping together. And as they lived, so they died—in the company of all family members—and were buried in family tombs.

In the worldview of the Ancient Near East, burial in the family grave serves to re-connect the spirit of the departed one with a realm of previously dead ancestors. This realm of departed beings was believed to exist within the region of the tomb itself or surrounding locality.[20] Given this assumption of postmortem existence, death was not regarded as an end point or cessation of existence. On the contrary, being gathered to one's ancestors implied a transition to another realm, one in which deceased family resided and activities of kith and kin continued within the sacred ancestral society of the family tomb. It is this understanding of the nature of death and the world beyond that inspires and drives the desire to be buried at Machpelah.[21] As Herbert Chanan Brichto suggests:

> [it is] not mere sentimental respect for the physical remains [that is] ... the motivation for the practice, but rather an assumed connection between proper sepulture and the condition of happiness of the deceased in the afterlife.[22]

Rachel's Death and the Transformation of a Symbol

Another Biblical motif of burial is found in the tale of Rachel's death. After a difficult, fatal childbirth, the Book of Genesis tells us: "Rachel died, and was buried on the way to Ephrath, which is Beth-Lehem. And Jacob set a pillar—*matzevah*—upon her grave, that is the pillar of Rachel's grave to this day. (Gen. 35:19-20).

This is the first instance in Biblical tradition of a formal grave-stone marker on someone's burial site. The word here, *matzevah*, is still used today when speaking of a cemetery tombstone. Erection of a pillar at Rachel's burial place has become the paradigm for the contemporary practice of erecting and unveiling a tombstone.[23]

1 Sam. 10:2 speaks of Rachel's tomb directly, indicating that in the time of the early monarchy, c. 1020 B.C.E., Rachel's tomb was a known landmark. More than four centuries later, as the citizens of Judah were exiled by the Babylonians, they were said to have passed by Rachel's tomb. In a well-known passage from the Book of Jeremiah, chanted as the second day Rosh HaShanah *Haftarah*, we read: "A voice was heard in Ramah, lamentation, and bitter weeping; Rachel weeping for her children." (Jer. 31:14) According to Midrash Rabbah, Jacob buried Rachel on the road south of Jerusalem so that future generations would pass her grave as they went into exile and she would be able to pray for them. (Gen. R. 82:10)

With her grave in Bethlehem, the Matriarch Rachel becomes a deceased spiritual intercessor on behalf of her Children, the People of Israel. In another Midrash (Lam. R. 24), we see a rather feisty and determined Matriarch Rachel arguing with God on behalf of the Children of Israel, who have been exiled to Babylonia:

> If I—a creature of flesh and blood, made of dust and ashes—could overcome my jealousy in order to be kind to my sister ... why are You, the sovereign of all existence, jealous of the false gods with whom the Israelites dally, false gods who aren't even real?! How can You let

Your jealousy cause your children to be slain and exiled?

In hearing "the sound of tears, weeping ... [and her] cries for her children" (Jer. 31:14), God responds to her pleas: "There is hope for your end of day ... the children will return to their borders." (Lam. R. 24)

While the precise geographical historicity is not so clear, traditions locating the tomb of *Rachel Emenu*—our Mother Rachel—just south of Jerusalem date back to c. 4th century C.E.[24] Over the course of centuries, Rachel's Tomb was transformed from a historical grave marker into a symbol of a mother weeping compassionately for her exiled children. Serving a dual role, Rachel's Tomb—*Kever Rachel*—became both a symbol of consolation for the pain of exile, and simultaneously, a symbol of hope, that one day the exile of Mother Rachel's Children will come to an end.

During the long exile of the Jewish people from the Land of Israel, it was Rachel's Tomb, more than any other visual symbol, that embodied the hope of the Return to the Land. Geography, psychological biography, and spiritual potency all converge in the story of Rachel and her grave-marker. As a younger sister, infertile wife, and mother who died in childbirth, Rachel knows the suffering of sibling rivalry, marital problems, infertility and tragic death. On the road to Bethlehem, to this day, Rachel's Tomb remains an archetypal beacon of light (not unlike the Statute of Liberty) providing guidance and consolation for the Jewish people in times of personal suffering and communal darkness. Tempered by the vicissitudes of life, *Kever Rachel* offers compassionate comfort, remedies of rescue and a hopeful promise for a better tomorrow.

Mummification — A Rare Act in Biblical Tradition

Rarely do we find descriptions of the ritual act of mummifying a corpse in Biblical tradition. However, there is clearly evidence of this occurring at the end of Genesis (50:2-3), where we read of how Joseph makes arrangements for the ritual preparation of his father Jacob's body:

> And Joseph commanded his servants, the physicians, to mummify—*la'hanot*—his father, and the physicians mummified—*va'yehantu*—Israel. And forty days were fulfilled for him; for so are fulfilled the days of those who are mummified—*yemei ha'hanutim*—and the Egyptians mourned for him seventy days.[25]

Joseph, being of high status among the Egyptians, was able to arrange for his father to have the traditional Egyptian preparations for burial. Similarly, when Joseph himself died, the last sentence of the Book of Genesis informs us: "Joseph died, being a hundred and ten years old; and they mummified him—*v'yehantu otoh*—and he was put in a coffin in Egypt." (Gen. 50:26)

According to the Egyptian view of the world beyond, each person had to have their individual body preserved intact for the afterlife. Traditions of the Egyptian Book of the Dead speak of an individual postmortem judgment and existence. In response to this philosophical worldview, the Egyptians developed a very unique and complex process of preservation of the physical body through embalming and mummification.[26]

The Hebrews, on the other hand, similar to the Canaanites, were buried in family tombs, and their individual mortal remains—"gathered to the ancestors," could upon decomposition blend, commingle and amalgamate with the bones of other family members, as they did in burial caves throughout the Ancient Near East.[27] While embalming was not, and to this day, is not a Jewish practice, there is nothing in the Jacob-Joseph cycle of Torah narratives, to indicate that this was a prohibited practice.[28] In his commentary on Genesis 50:2, Rashi, in a very prosaic way, with no further explanation, interprets *la'hanot* as being "a matter of mixing spices"—a reference to the idea that the process of mummification entailed coating the body with a mixture of preservative spices.[29]

However, in a Midrashic text (Gen. R. 100:3), Rabbi Yahuda expresses a Rabbinic concern about mummification, and explains that Joseph died earlier than his brothers "because he mummified his father."

The last chapter of Genesis goes on to describe ritual practices of the mummification process indicating "forty days were fulfilled for him; for so are fulfilled the days of those who are mummified; and the Egyptians mourned for him seventy days." (Gen. 50:3) These two distinct time frames—forty days and seventy days—correspond with what is known of Egyptian mummification practices.

According to Rachel Hallote:

> The entire mourning process took seventy days, exactly the time that the Egyptians mourned Jacob. But the most important part of the embalming process was the time the body spent drying out in the natron [a sodium chloride and sodium sulphate based embalming solution] the time specified for embalming in the Biblical passage quoted above. The Egyptians mourned Jacob from the moment he died until his mummy was complete, as they would mourn any Egyptian,

because Jacob's mortuary treatment was completely Egyptian.[30]

While this kind of preparation for burial would not have been required in any way by Jewish practice, given Jacob's request to be buried at Machpelah, mummification was necessary for the long trek back to Canaan in the desert heat.

Jacob's Funeral Cortege

After Jacob's body was completely prepared for burial, in the style of Egyptian funerary culture, plans could then be made to transport his remains back to Canaan. The next thing Joseph had to do was secure permission from Pharaoh so that he, his brothers, and their accompanying household entourage, could leave Egypt and sojourn back to Hebron with Jacob's sarcophagus. "The difficulty was not only that even a high official such as Joseph did not have freedom of movement, but also one of explaining to Pharaoh why his father would not have considered it a privilege to be buried in Egypt."[31]

Under what circumstances would Pharaoh have agreed to send a Hebrew-Egyptian retinue to Canaan and back? After all, at least from the Egyptian point of view, ancient Egyptian culture had an exceptionally sophisticated and evolved technology for guaranteeing successful passage from this realm to the world beyond. Why should Joseph have to transport his father anywhere else for burial? Even more: considering the desert climate and terrain, this was not a journey to be undertaken lightly, without adequate supplies and preparation. Had not Jacob spent the last seventeen years of his life enjoying the cultural ambiance of life in Egypt? Would not an Egyptian burial be simpler and more dignified than a long trek through the hot Sinai desert?

Yet Joseph had taken an oath to honor his father's deathbed wishes. Hence he had little choice but to issue a petitionary appeal to Pharaoh:

> And when the days of his mourning were past, Joseph spoke to the house of Pharaoh, saying, "If now I have found grace in your eyes, speak, I beg you, in the ears of Pharaoh, saying, 'My father made me swear, saying, *Behold, I die; in my grave which I have dug for me in the land of Canaan, there shall you bury me.* Now therefore let me go up, I beg you, and bury my father, and I will return.'" And Pharaoh said, "Go up, and bury your father, according as he made you swear." (Gen. 50:4-5)

Interestingly, in his request to Pharaoh, Joseph adds one piece of information that was not in Jacob's original deathbed communication, and nowhere in the earlier descriptions of Machpelah. Joseph claims, in Jacob's voice, that his father wishes to buried "in my grave which *I have dug for myself* in Canaan." (Gen. 50:5) But this was simply not true: we can assume the burial cave at Machpelah had been intact since the time of his grandfather Abraham; but neither Abraham, Isaac nor Jacob himself ever allude to the need to dig out the specific place for their own burial. However, it seems this slight exaggeration is exactly the rationale required to guarantee the permission to travel from Pharaoh. Given the pre-occupation Egyptian Pharaohs had "building monumental tombs for themselves to ensure their immortality, [Pharaoh] could be expected to sympathize with an individual who desired to be buried in the tomb on which he had expended time and resources to build for himself."[32]

Joseph's slight exaggeration of the truth worked; in reply to his request, he received a simple and clear communication from Pharaoh granting him permission to travel: "And Pharaoh said, 'Go up, and bury your father, according as he made you swear.'" (Gen. 50:6)

Next, the text describes Jacob's funeral cortege—seemingly a grand retinue of people and livestock, Joseph's brothers, their families and herds, accompanying Egyptian royal servants, as well as chariots and horsemen all escorting Jacob's bier on the route from Goshen towards Hebron:

And Joseph went up to bury his father; and with him went up all the servants of Pharaoh, the elders of his house, and all the elders of the land of Egypt, and all the house of Joseph, and his brothers, and his father's house; only their little ones, and their flocks, and their herds, they left in the land of Goshen. And there went up with him both chariots and horsemen; and it was a very great company. (Gen. 50:7-9)

From the description here, it appears Joseph and his retinue are enacting a ritual procession as they traverse from Egypt to Canaan, ultimately taking a circuitous route,[33] crossing over the Jordan River (Gen. 50:11) and eventually landing at Atad.

In Genesis 50:12-13, we read of Jacob's successful arrival in Canaan, and that "his sons did to him according as he commanded them; for his sons carried him to the land of Canaan." According to Midrash Genesis Rabbah, Jacob had specifically requested he be transported to Canaan in a unique ritual formation, his coffin surrounded on each of the four directions by groups of three of his sons:

Set this arrangement for me: Three of you carry me on the north of the bier, three on the south side, three on the east side, and three on the west side. And just as you are doing this for me now, so you are destined to do in the future, travel in four formations in the Wilderness [of Sinai] in the four directions of the compass, three tribes in each formation, with you the Shechinah in the center (Gen. R. 100.2).[34]

His sons Reuben, Simeon, Judah, Issachar, Zebulun, Naftali, Asher, Gad, Dan, Benjamin, and his grandsons Ephraim and Menasseh were the coffin-bearers. Joseph, because of his high status, and Levi because of his priestly role were both exempt from this task (Rashi on Gen. 50:13).

However, according to Schubert Spero, author of "The Funeral of Jacob: A Joint Hebrew-Egyptian Affair," what is evidenced in the processional description in Genesis replicates Egyptian funerary practices that included elaborate ritualistic processional ceremonies prior to burial.[35] Description of an Egyptian funeral ritual seems to corroborate this idea:

The transport of the body to the tomb took the form of a ritual procession normally beginning on the east bank of the Nile and crossing over on ferries to the cemeteries on the west ... [C]lose to the mummy stood two women impersonating the divine mourners Isis and Nephthys ... then followed by groups of mourning women ... As the bier [neared the tomb it] was greeted by ritual dancers as a lector-priestess read from a papyrus [of] funerary spells in honor of the deceased.[36]

We next read in the Genesis narrative that Jacob's funeral cortege arrived at the "threshing floor of Atad, which is beyond the Jordan":

> ... and there they mourned with a great and bitter lamentation; and he made a mourning for his father seven days. And when the inhabitants of the land, the Canaanites, saw the mourning in the floor of Atad, they said, "This is a grievous mourning to the Egyptians"; therefore the name of it was called Abel-Mizraim, which is beyond the Jordan. (Gen. 50:10-11)

Spero again associates these rituals in the Genesis story with Egyptian funerary practices, noting how—as quoted above—in ancient Egypt "as the bier [neared the tomb it] was greeted by ritual dancers as a lector-priestess read from a papyrus [of] funerary spells in honor of the deceased."[37] This ritualized communal mourning activity, according to Spero, required a flat open area—and the threshing floor at Atad served that purpose perfectly providing the location where final Egyptian funerary rites were administered. The pomp and circumstance of a large retinue of mourners—and there is no doubt there were loud wails of mourning women as would have been customary at that time—made a deep impression on the local inhabitants. Hence, Atad was given the name *Abel-Mizraim*—the mourning of Egypt.

Subsequently, the Genesis text tell us, Joseph and his brothers buried Jacob "in the cave of the field of Machpelah, which Abraham bought with the field for a possession of a burying place of Ephron the Hittite, before Mamre." (Gen. 50:13) Even though there had not yet been a clear reconciliation between Joseph and his brothers, all the sons, whether estranged or alienated, disgruntled or criticized, were able to gather together in fulfillment of their father Jacob's last requests. In his death, the children of Jacob were once again united as family, on the soil of the Land of Israel, to honor their obligations to bury their father.

Finally, for the Rabbis of Palestine, who wrote the early *midrashim*, their concern was not to understand the obscured minutiae of Egyptian death rituals that may have been hidden in layers of the Biblical text. For them, writing almost 1,500 years later, they needed to understand the story of Jacob's death and burial in ways that were confluent with their own view of the world. Using Midrash as a tool of interpretation, the question they asked was why Jacob, and all the Patriarchs, expressed such strong desire to be buried back in the Land of Israel.

One teaching, in the name of Rabbi Helbo, was: "Because the dead of Eretz Israel will be the first to be resurrected in the days of the Messiah and to enjoy the years of the Messiah." (Gen. R. 96:4) Taking this one step further, Resh Lakish taught that when the Patriarchs reach the Land of Israel "God will put a soul into them, for it says, "He gives a soul to the people spirit to those who walk [on the earth]." (Isa. 42:5) (Gen. R. 96:4)

We have here the doctrine of the resurrection of the dead, in Hebrew, *tehiyat ha'metim*[38]—a belief that the dead will live again at some future time, be united with their physical bodies, and participate in the triumph of a divine messianic kingdom on earth. Resurrection became a central doxology in Judaism, and while central to the Rabbinic worldview, an exploration of this topic will take us far beyond our present scope of inquiry.[39]

However, to conclude this section on Jacob's death, there is one more vignette. In response to Rabbi Helbo, Rabbi Simon asked, what happens to the righteous who are buried outside the Land of Israel? He answered:

> What does God do? He makes cavities like channels for them in the earth, and they roll along in them until they reach the Land of Israel, when the Holy One, blessed be He, will infuse into them a spirit of life and they will arise. How do we know this? Because it is

written, "Behold, I will open your graves, and cause you to come up out of your graves, O My people; and I will bring you into the land of Israel." (Ezek. 37:12) (Gen. R. 96:4)

This concept of souls rolling through the earth to get to the Land of Israel is known in Rabbinic tradition. The idea is that since the resurrection of the dead will begin in the Holy Land, being buried outside of Israel is an impediment to being resurrected and participating in God's messianic kingdom. Interestingly, this idea has left a trace on customs of Jewish ritual practice. To this day in traditional Jewish burial preparation outside of Israel, members of the *Hevra Kaddisha*, the burial society, sprinkle a packet of earth from Mount of Olives upon the *met*, the body of the deceased. This earth is seen as symbolic way of connecting the dead person to the land of Israel where the resurrection will begin. Additionally, in another ritual that is *minhag* not *halakhah*—custom not law—in traditional Jewish burial preparation small twigs are placed in the casket, sometimes right in the hand of the deceased. For what purpose? So that at the time of the resurrection the deceased may be able to burrow through the earth to get to Jerusalem to participate in the resurrection of the dead and the emerging messianic kingdom.

Biblical legend, Midrashic interpretation, Jewish philosophical teachings on afterlife and eschatology, and Jewish ritual practices on death, burial and mourning are all inter-woven. The story of Jacob's death in Egypt and burial at Machpelah is a multi-textured tradition and provides much opportunity for learning and exploration.

Joseph's Bones

Another motif associated with burial in Jewish tradition is that of "Joseph's bones." After returning home from burying his father in Canaan, and subsequently attempting to make peace with his brothers, we read of Joseph's dying request:

> I am dying, but God will take account of you, and will bring you up from this land to the land which he swore to Abraham, to Isaac, and to Jacob. Joseph had the Children of Israel swear, saying: When God takes account of you, bring my bones up from here. And Joseph died, being a hundred and ten years old. (Gen. 50:24 –25)

After an enigmatic life-journey of trauma, tribulation and adventure, the days of Joseph the dreamer, Jacob's beloved son and the esteemed advisor to the Egyptian Pharaoh, finally come to an end. However, unlike his father Jacob, Joseph does not ask his surviving kinfolk to transport him to

Canaan immediately after death. Instead, on his deathbed he speaks of a future era when God will bring all the Hebrews out of Egypt. When that redemption takes place, he says to his brothers, "you shall carry up my bones up from here" (Gen. 50:25) to Canaan, land of his birth. This is Joseph's end-of-life entreaty, one final petition to his brothers with whom he had a complex relationship and destiny. Subsequently, with Joseph dead and his body mummified and encased in an Egyptian coffin, the Book of Genesis reaches its grand finale (Gen. 50:26) and the Patriarchal era of Biblical history comes to an end.

However, the motif of "Joseph's bones" continues for centuries in Biblical tradition. It appears twice more in the narratives of the Hebrew Bible, and is explored extensively in Midrash. In the Book of Exodus we once again hear of "Joseph's bones." After suffering the hardships of slavery under "the king who knew not Joseph" (Ex. 1:8), the Israelites are eventually freed from the grasp of Egyptian oppression. Amidst the chaos of moving a wild and wooly slave nation out of Egypt, their charismatic leader Moses "had taken Joseph's bones with him; for he had made the Children of Israel swear, yes swear, saying ... bring my bones up from here with you." (Ex. 13:19)

Throughout the ensuing forty years of desert wandering, nothing more is said in the Biblical text about "Joseph's bones." Eventually, after

Moses' death, Joshua leads the Israelite military conquest of Canaan; subsequently, Joshua dies, and only then do "Joseph's bones" reappear for the third and final time. Joshua 24:31 informs us that "the elders who outlived Joshua" attend to the Joseph's final burial in Shechem:

> And the bones of Joseph, which the Children of Israel brought out of Egypt, they buried in Shechem, in a parcel of ground which Jacob bought from the sons of Hamor the father of Shechem for a hundred pieces of silver; and it became the inheritance of the sons of Joseph. (Josh. 24:32)

The nature of Midrash is that it clarifies contradictions in the Biblical text and also seeks to provide answers to confusing or unknown dimensions of Torah narratives. With regard to Joseph's bones, Midrashic tradition elaborates extensively upon the Biblical material, addressing two central questions: first of all, where exactly were "Joseph's bones" during the centuries of slavery in Egypt? And secondly, how was Moses able to find the location where Joseph's coffin had been placed?

Regarding the whereabouts of "Joseph's bones" (according to Deut. R. 11:7), Joseph's coffin had been hidden by the Egyptians in order to prevent the Hebrews from leaving Egypt. However, like a mythic character on the Hero's Quest, needing to overcome unending trials and tribulations, Moses fervently searches for Joseph's coffin and the bones hidden therein.

According to Mekhilta of Rabbi Yishmael (and other *midrashim)* Sera<u>h</u> bat Asher, Jacob's granddaughter, the longest-living survivor from Joseph's generation, knew exactly where her Uncle Joseph's coffin had been hidden. According to Midrashic tradition, as a wise old woman, she was able to help Moses discover the specific location where Joseph's bones were to be found, submerged beneath the Nile:

> It is told that Sera<u>h</u>, the daughter of Asher survived from that generation and she showed Moses the grave of Joseph. She said to him: The Egyptians put him in a small metal coffin which they sunk in the Nile. So Moses went and stood by the Nile. He took a table[t] of gold on which he engraved the Tetragrammaton, and throwing it into the Nile, he cried out and said: "Joseph son of Jacob! The oath to redeem his children, which God swore to our father Abraham, has reached its fulfillment." Immediately Joseph's coffin came up to the surface, and Moses took it. (Mekhilta, Beshalach, 2)

Another Midrashic text, Midrash Ha'Gadol,

delineates a fascinating methodology used by Moses for elevating Joseph's coffin from Nile:

> Moses took Joseph's goblet and cut four pieces out of it. On one he drew a lion, on another an ox, on another an eagle, and on another a man. [Then] he stood at the Nile, threw [in] the image of the lion, and said: "Joseph, the time has come for Israel to be redeemed"; but [the coffin] did not rise. He threw in the drawing of the ox, and then of the eagle, but it did not rise. [Finally] he threw in the drawing of the man and said, "Joseph, the time has come." Joseph's coffin immediately floated to the top of the water, and Moses took it. (Midrash Ha'Gadol, end of Genesis)

What is interesting here is the mythic resonance between the Joseph story and the Egyptian myth of Isis and Osiris. Osiris, an Egyptian deity, connected with the Nile, was a King of Egypt, who ruled with his wife beloved, Isis, as Queen. Killed by his jealous brother Set, Osiris was dismembered and thrown into the river in a coffin. Bereft of her husband, Isis went off in search of Osiris.[40] Using her magical powers, Isis was able to gather up the fourteen parts of his body from the waters of the Nile, thus resurrecting Osiris—a process quite identical to the one described in Midrash Ha'Gadol, a Midrashic compilation dating from the 14th century C.E.

Other *midrashim* maintain that because of the loyalty Moses demonstrated in searching for Joseph's bones at the time of the Exodus, he alone merited the unprecedented honor of being buried by God upon his own death. (Deut. 34:6) In the days prior to the departure from Egypt, while the Israelites were greedily gathering booty of silver and gold, Moses would have none of that, and instead embarked upon a passionate search for Joseph's bones. According to Deuteronomy Rabbah:

> And while Israel carried the silver and gold which they had taken away from Egypt, Moses was carrying Joseph's coffin. God said to him: "Moses, you say that you have done a small thing; by your life, this act of kindness is a great thing; since as you ignored silver and gold, I too will do unto you this kindness in that I will busy Myself with your burial." (Deut. R. 11:7)

Once out of Egypt, the Israelites carried Joseph's bones on the trek through Sinai with a reverential sense of the sacred. According to the Babylonian Talmud, both the bones of Joseph, and the Ark of the Covenant were carried by the Israelites side-by-side through the wilderness:

All those years that the Israelites were in the wilderness, those two chests, one of the dead and the other of the Shekhinah, proceeded side by side, and passersby used to ask: "What is the nature of those two chests?" They received the reply: "One is of the dead and the other of the Shekhinah." "But is it, then, the way of the dead to proceed with the Shekhinah?" They were told, "This one [Joseph] fulfilled all that was written in the other." (Sotah 13a-13b)

For the Israelites on their forty-year long desert journey, Joseph's bones are not an after-thought, a residue from ancient days transported with a sense of habituated duty, and nothing more. Instead, just like the Ark of the Covenant and the Ten Commandments contained therein, the ritual carrying of Joseph's bones are in a sense essential to the spiritual foundation of the nation. In complying with Joseph's deathbed request to "bring my bones up from here with you" (Ex. 13:19), for the wandering Israelites, the Sinai journey becomes simultaneously both a pilgrimage to freedom, as well as a national funeral procession honoring the dead,[41] that, at one and the same time, carries forth the legacy of the ancestors.

Eventually, after Moses dies, Joshua and the Israelites traverse the Jordan, and the newly inaugurated Israelite leader is preoccupied with military and political affairs, and the challenges of settling the land. However, upon Joshua's death, those elders who survive (Josh. 24:31) make arrangements for the final internment of Joseph's bones at Shechem.

And why is Shechem the site of Joseph's final burial asks the Midrash? According to Exodus Rabbah: "it was from Shechem that the brothers of Joseph had [first] stolen him and had him sold" (Ex. R. 20:19). Joseph's life journey comes full circle and, in the end, Joseph's bones are returned to Shechem and to the land of Israel where they are said to remain to this day.

Today, the Cave of Machpelah, Rachel's Tomb and Joseph's Tomb, are all pilgrimage sights in contemporary Israel. They are living symbols and reminders of how Judaism honors the lives and deaths of our Biblical ancestors.

BIBLICAL MOURNING PRACTICES

Terms Describing Types of Mourning in Biblical Tradition

IN THE HEBREW BIBLE, we find a plethora of descriptions and depictions of rites and rituals related to mourning for the dead. Ritual practices include, but are not limited to: rending one's garment, wearing sackcloth, sitting on the ground, covering one's self with dirt, fasting, weeping, wailing and singing dirges of mourning.[42] Along with different lengths of time associated with mourning, there are also different terms used to talk about ways of mourning, suggesting that there were varied types and qualities of mourning. Terms used most frequently are: 1) *lispod*—to mourn, or lament; 2) *livkot*—to weep, to wail; and 3) *evel*, mourning—a noun rather than a verb, suggesting a mourning event or experience.

In Genesis 23:1, the first two terms are used together—upon the death of his wife Sarah: "Abraham came to mourn—*lispod*—for Sarah and to weep for her—*livkotah*." The word, *livkot*, connotes weeping and wailing, and has the quality of an intensity of tears. This term is also used for the deaths of both Aaron and Moses. In describing communal reactions to the deaths of Moses and Aaron, the specific term is *va'yivku*—"And the people of Israel wept—*va'yivku*—for Moses in the plains of Moab thirty days." (Deut. 34:8) And after thirty days: "the days of weeping—*yemei behi* (a variant form of *va'yivku*)—and mourning for Moses were ended." (Ibid.) Similarly, according to Numbers 20:28: "and they mourned—*va'yivku*—for Aaron thirty days."

The second term—*lispod*—is from the verbal root *safad*, which means to lament.[43] While today we used the term *hesped* to refer to a verbal eulogy delivered at a funeral, here the word *lispod*, has a different connotation as a very active type of tearful, vocal mourning. The term appears elsewhere in Torah, used to speak of how Joseph and his family mourned Jacob in Canaan. According to Genesis 50:10: "and there they mourned —*va'yispedu*—a great and bitter lamentation—*misped gadol*." In this passage, there is a quality of intensity in this form of mourning. The Amoraic sage Ulla said: "The technical meaning of *hesped* is lamenting with striking upon the breast." (MK 27b) Bar suggests that *lispod* may be a bitter cry similar to a dirge or lament, perhaps lasting a full day.[44]

A third term for mourning is *evel*. In Genesis 50:10, we read: "And they came to the threshing floor of Atad ... and there they mourned with a great and bitter lamentation; and he made a mourning—*evel*—for his father seven days."

Because the Bible as a whole depicts the cultural history of the Israelites spanning more than a millennium of time, there is never a consistent use of any specific language to describe mourning, and the wide diversity of rituals likely reflects different eras and communities of Jewish life.[45]

Mourning For Seven Days

The singularly most important time frame for mourning in Jewish tradition is the seven-day period immediately following a death, which has come to be known as the period of *Shiva*. This practice of observing seven days of ritualized mourning goes back very far into the recesses of Biblical and Rabbinic cultural history.

In the Torah, the first use of seven days of mourning is associated with Jacob's death. After the Hebrew-Egyptian entourage arrived at Atad, in Canaan, Joseph and his brothers "mourned with a great and bitter lamentation; and [Joseph] made a mourning for his father seven days." (Gen. 50:7) As noted, the term used in the text here is *evel*. Similarly, after burying Saul and his sons residents of Jabesh-Gilead "fasted for seven days." (1 Sam. 31:13) And Job's friends "sat down with him on the ground seven days and seven nights"

(Job 2:13) comforting him in his loss.

There are a few instances that reveal shorter periods of mourning. When Saul and Jonathan, and their troops were killed in battle on Mt. Gilboa (2 Sam. 1:12), David and his men only observed one day of mourning—they "mourned, and wept, and fasted until the evening ... because they had fallen by the sword." Similarly, following the death of Abner, David mourned until the end of the day (2 Sam. 3:35), although one can read nuances in the Biblical to suggest that the fighting men of David's army ceased mourning even before that first day ended.[46]

There are also two instances of the mourning period being longer than seven days. For both Aaron (Num. 20:29) and for Moses (Deut. 34:8), the Israelites observed thirty days of mourning. We can assume the longer mourning period here was because they were important community leaders.[47] But overall and most consistently in Biblical tradition, seven days is the usual time of mourning.

By the time of the Second Temple, the seven-day mourning period had become standard practice. According to the Apocryphal text Wisdom of Ben Sira, dating from the 2nd century B.C.E., "Mourning for the dead last seven days." (Ben Sira 22:12) However, because the Joseph narrative took place before the revelation at Sinai, the Rabbis were reluctant to infer from Joseph's practice of seven days of mourning for his father a rationale for the halakhic practice of seven days of mourning. Hence, in their consistent style, the Rabbis tried to find other proof-text rationales for a seven day period of mourning.

To give credibility to the seven-day practice, the Jerusalem Talmud (Ket. 1,1) asserts that Moses instituted the practice of both seven days of mourning after a death, and seven days of celebration after a marriage. The theme of seven days of mourning is discussed extensively in Midrash Genesis Rabbah (100:7). Here is the transcript of the conversation of seven different Rabbis, each coming up with a different proof text to rationalize the tradition of seven days of mourning:

According to Resh Lakish [the proof text was]: "And you shall not go out from the door of the tent of meeting seven days" (Lev. 8:13): even as you were anointed seven days with the oil of anointing, so do you keep seven days [of mourning] for your brethren.

According to R. Hoshaya [the proof text was]: "And at the door of the tent of meeting you shall abide day and night seven days, and keep the observance of the Lord" (Lev. 8:35): as the Lord observed seven days [of mourning] for His world, so must you keep seven days for your brethren.

According to R. Joshua b. Levi: Seven days did the Holy One, blessed be He, mourn for His world (after the Flood).

According to R. Johanan [the proof text was]: "Let her not, I pray, be as one dead, but instead, let her be shut up seven days" (Num. 12:12, 14): as the days of shutting up are seven so are the days of mourning seven.

According to R. Abbahu [the proof text was]: "Let her not, I pray, be as one dead" (Num. 12:12): as the days of [defilement through] the dead are seven, so are the days of [defilement for] definite leprosy seven.'

According to R. Jeremiah and R. Hiyya b. Abba [the proof text was]: "And I will turn your feasts into mourning" (Amos 8:10). As the days of the Feast (*hag*) are seven, so are the days of mourning seven.

This kind of discourse demonstrates how the Rabbis were evolving a system of death practices, and continually struggled to ground these practices in texts of Torah. Over time, other Rabbinic sources such as Moed Katan and Semahot institutionalized the diversity of ritual practices related to death, dying and mourning.[48] But the above quote demonstrates how the Rabbis of the Babylonian Talmud, aspired to establish a connection between the Patriarchal traditions of Torah and the later evolution of Jewish ritual practice.

Rending Garments and Donning Sackcloth

One mourning practice occurring repeatedly in the Bible is the ritual act of tearing one's garment at the time of death. This is first mentioned in the Book of Genesis: upon returning to the pit where his brothers had placed Joseph, and discovering he was no longer there, Reuben assumed Joseph was dead, and "he tore his clothes." (Gen. 37:29) Similarly, when Jacob is told Joseph has been devoured by an animal, "Jacob tore his clothes ... and mourned for his son many days" (Gen. 37:34) Upon hearing news of the death of his children, "Job arose and tore his robe ... and fell down upon the ground ... (Job 1:20); and after being defeated in battle by the fighting men at Ai, "Joshua tore his clothes, and fell to the earth upon his face before the Ark of the Lord until the evening, he and the elders of Israel, and [in a related ritual] put dust upon their heads." (Josh. 7:6)[49]

Another practice closely associated with rending

one's garments is donning sackcloth. In addition to tearing his clothes upon news of Joseph's death, Jacob also "put sackcloth upon his loins" (Gen. 37:34); and when King David was burying and mourning Abner, he instructed the people "Tear your clothes, and gird yourself with sackcloth." (2 Sam. 3:31)

There also is textual evidence that some kind of specific mourning garb was worn. In 2 Samuel 14:2: "Joab sent to Tekoah, and fetched there a wise woman, and said to her, 'I beg you, feign yourself to be a mourner, and put on now a mourning dress, and anoint not yourself with oil, but be as a woman that has for a long time mourned for the dead.'" Elsewhere, we read of how Tamar "took off her widow's garments" (Gen. 38:14), although we have no idea of what those garments would have consisted.

Unlike burial practices, which can leave some form of archaeological remnants, we have no material evidence from ancient mourning practices. So we are left utilizing textual and theoretical conjecture to fully understand the context of ancient mourning practices.[50]

Clearly symbolic use of clothing was part of how ancient Biblical Israelites experienced and demonstrated grief. Bar suggests the ritual of tearing one's garment may be a symbolic substitute for self-mutilation, or perhaps a "relic of an ancient custom in which mourners bared their chest."[51] Regardless of the obscure, misty origins of this practice in Ancient Near Eastern culture, undoubtedly there is historical precedent for having one's garments express outwardly one's inner state of bereavement.

According to the *Shulhan Arukh*, the Code of Jewish Law (Yoreh Deah, Ch. 340),[52] to this day it is halachically prescribed to rend one's garment through the ritual act of *keriah*, literally "tearing" or "ripping." While some people do observe this ritual, in contemporary Jewish life we have sanitized the practice of tearing one's garments as a demonstration of mourning. Today, at a funeral mourners are pinned with a black button with a ribbon attached and torn symbolically, said to represent the torn heart of grief. But the traditional practice—as the Torah indicates— is, and always has been literally ripping of one's clothing, designed to express a catharsis of emotions of grief and pain. An understanding of the Biblical origins of this practice may motivate contemporary mourners to consider performing the more traditional form of this practice.[53]

Sitting on the Floor

Another ritual practice connected with mourning in Biblical times is sitting on the floor. We see this in a number of texts, including: "Then all the princes of the sea shall come down from their thrones and lay away their robes, and take off their embroidered garments; they shall dress themselves with trembling; they shall sit upon the ground" (Ezek. 26:16); "And he took a potsherd with which to scrape himself; and he sat down among the ashes" (Job 2:8); "And her gates shall lament and mourn; and she being desolate shall sit upon the ground" (Isa. 3:26); and after David is informed of the death of his sons, he "arose, and tore his garments, and lay on the earth" (2 Sam. 13:31).

This theme is found in numerous other texts, as well as in contemporaneous non-Biblical sources of the ancient world. For example, in Canaanite sacred poetry, God, in response to the death of Baal, "descends from the throne, sits on the footstool; and from the footstool, and sits on the ground."[54]

Bar suggests sitting on the ground "was a sign of humility and of identification with the dead, but also of proximity to the underworld."[55] Today we no longer sit on the ground in times of mourning, though the Jewish tradition of sitting on lowered stools during the week of *Shiva* is a ritual remnant of this ancient practice which embodies in a very physical and concretized way the emotional state of mourning.

Weeping and Silence

In ancient Biblical tradition, as we read in the Book of Ecclesiastes, there is a recognition that there is "a time to weep, and a time to laugh; a time to mourn ... a time to keep silence, and a time to speak." (Ecc. 3:7, 10) Certainly in houses of mourning today, we often encounter weeping and laughter as well as both silence and speaking. And this juxtaposition of weeping and silence is documented in the Hebrew Bible.[56]

When Sarah died, Abraham mourned and wept for her (Gen. 23:2); the children of Israel wept for Moses when he died on the plains of Moab (Num. 25:6) and Joash the King of Israel wept when the Prophet Elisha became sick and was to die. (2 Kings 13:14)

In the Book of Job, we read that Job's friends, as they came to comfort in his time of loss, "lifted up their voice and wept; and they sat down with him on the ground seven days and seven nights, and no one spoke a word to him; for they saw that his suffering was very great." (Job 2:12-13)

In later Rabbinic tradition, this passage was seen as a textual basis for the practice of not speaking to offer consolation to a mourner until the one in mourning first speaks. According to Moed Katan 28b: "Comforters are not permitted to say a word until the mourner opens conversation." And in

Berakhot 6b, Rav Papa extols the virtue of silence, teaching that "the merit of attending a house of mourning lies in the silence observed."

Today many are often uncomfortable in a house of mourning, uncertain how to best respond to a mourner, unsure of what to say. Out of anxiety we often fear the emptiness of silence. Yet as we see here, Biblical tradition teaches us to honor the value of silence as a way of being with mourners.

Dirges and Wailing Women

Another practice of mourning in Biblical times was the dirge or lament, in Hebrew *kinah*. Dirges—Hebrew plural *kinot*[57] were sung as part of funerary ritual, and extolled virtues of the deceased.[58] For example, upon the death of King Saul and Jonathan, David, a musician and poet, offered a lament declaring how "Saul and Jonathan were loved and dear in their lives … they were swifter than eagles, they were stronger than lions." (2 Sam. 1:23) And at the death of Abner, David sang a funeral lament on his behalf (2 Sam. 3:31ff.) that caused those present to "weep again over him." (2 Sam. 3:34)

As a rule, dirges were sung by professionally-trained vocalists hired to weep and sing laments on behalf of the deceased. Their task was "not only to perform mourning in context of death or calamity, but to draw out the appropriate ritual response from others gathered to mourn."⁵⁹

In 2 Chronicles 35:24, we read about *sharim* and *sharot*—male singers and female singers—who, along with Jeremiah offered lamentations at the time of the death of King Josiah. Elsewhere, evidence suggests that it was predominantly a guild of women who were educated specifically for the task of singing laments as part of ancient funerary practice:

According to Jeremiah 9:16-19:

> Thus says the Lord of hosts, Consider, and call for the mourning women—*mekonenot*—that they may come; and send for skilled women —*ḥokhamot*—that they may come; and let them make haste, and take up a wailing for us, that our eyes may run down with tears, and our eyelids gush out with waters. For a voice of wailing is heard out of Zion ... Yet hear the word of the Lord, O you women, and let your ear receive the word of his mouth, and teach your daughters wailing, and every one her neighbor lamentation.

These *mekonenot*—female dirge-singers—"were expert in their craft, trained to sing or compose funeral songs, [and] passed their special skills from generation to generation."⁶⁰

By the early Rabbinic era, the practice of hiring

professional dirge singers at a funeral was formally institutionalized. A married man was supposed to provide for the burial needs of his wife, and "even the poorest man in Israel must provide no less than two flutes and one lamenting woman." (M. Ket. 4:4)

Texts indicate that playing of the flute was also part of ancient Jewish funeral practice. This is evidenced further in the New Testament: "When Jesus came to the leader's house, he saw the flute players and a crowd lamenting loudly" (Matt. 9:23); and another Jewish source speaks of hiring flute players "for a bride and for [the funeral of] the dead." (M. BM 6:1)

While the notion of flute accompaniment and women singing dirges at funeral seems foreign to our contemporary sense of normative Jewish practice, it is clear that these practices were once an integral part of ancient Jewish mourning rituals.

The exploration of Biblical mourning rituals presented in this chapter demonstrates that Jewish mourning and funerary practices have evolved and continue to be evolving. Perhaps in a spirit of renewal of ancient traditions it is appropriate to consider bringing back into practice use of lament, dirge singing and musical accompaniment at contemporary Jewish funerals.

MOSES' DEATH
AND THE STAGES OF DYING

THIS CHAPTER EXPLORES the motif of Moses' death. In particular, I examine ways in which Moses responds to the reality of his impending death, as documented in Torah and a series of accompanying *midrashim*.

Textually, there are more variant Midrashic traditions on Moses' death than on any other deathbed narrative in Jewish tradition. As a consequence, the various Biblical and Midrashic texts provide a rich model to explore the complex process people go through in grappling with the approach of death. In a sense, Moses' death—said to be caused by a "kiss from God"—is the ideal model for people to strive for. Through a mélange of creative Midrashic traditions on Moses' death, we are guided and invited to think about our own personal and cultural attitudes towards the experience and process of dying.

Moses' Death in Torah

Early in the book of Deuteronomy, Moses is informed that he will die without realizing his life-long dream of entering the Promised Land. We find a rather curt dialogue between Moses and

God: "Please let me cross the Jordan River," Moses pleads, "Let me see the wonderful Promised Land, the beautiful hills, and the mountains of Lebanon across the Jordan." (Deut. 3:25)

This is not at all an unreasonable request from a man who dedicated his life herding an unruly mass of 600,000 souls from the dregs of Egyptian slavery toward a land flowing with milk and honey. But his aspirations to cross the River Jordan were not to be fulfilled, because: "The Lord was angry at me, and would not listen. The Lord angrily told me, 'That is enough! Do not speak to Me any more about My decision.'" (Deut. 3:26) Essentially, God tells Moses: 'This issue is non-negotiable! I am not going to speak with you about your death any more. It's a done deal!' Once decreed by God, there was to be no further protest or rebuttal from Moses.

However, in an act of compassion and mercy, God does permit Moses a temporary glimpse of the Land—"You can climb to top of Mount Pisgah, and look West, North, South, and East. Take a good look" ... but Moses gets just a glance of the Promised Land and nothing more: "because you will not cross the Jordan River." It will be his successor Joshua, and not Moses, who will bring the people into the Land. (Deut. 3:27-28)

Further on in Deuteronomy, we see how Moses shares this news with the entire Israelite nation, stating quite simply: "I must die on this side of the

Jordan River, but you will be the ones to cross over and occupy the Promised Land." (Deut. 4:22) From this text, we are left with the impression that Moses accepts his fate with composure and equanimity. It appears to be the end of the matter; there is no further discussion on the topic. Moses is going to die—that's it! Even as we move towards the closing chapters of Deuteronomy, Moses reviews his life, and with a sense of silent acceptance he says nothing more about his approaching death. It seems like a done deal.

And in the closing verses of Deuteronomy 32, God once more reminds Moses of his fate:

> Climb Mount Avarim, to Mount Nebo, in the land of Moab, facing Jericho; and see the land of Canaan, I am giving the Israelites as an inheritance; you will die on the mountain that you are climbing, and be gathered to your people ... you shall see the land from afar; but you shall not go there to the land ...(Deut. 32: 49-50; 52)

A reading of these Torah texts reveals absolutely no protestations whatsoever from Moses, nor any emotional or existential angst about his impending end of life. It is obvious that Moses had effectively been silenced much earlier.

As the story of Moses—Moshe ben Amram v'Yocheved—winds down to its final conclusion, with the factual nostalgia of a newspaper obituary, at the end of Deuteronomy we are told:

> So Moses the servant of the Lord died there in the land of Moab, according to the word of the Lord. And he buried him in a valley in the land of Moab, opposite Beth-Peor; but no man knows his grave till this day. And Moses was one hundred and twenty years old when he died; his eye was not dim, nor his natural force abated. (Deut. 34:5-7)

While the Torah does report on the grief of the Israelite people—"For thirty days the Israelites mourned Moses on the plains of Moab" (Deut. 34:8) —there is nothing whatsoever in Deuteronomy that reveals any sense of Moses' own reaction to the inevitability of his death, east of the Jordan. Uncharacteristically, in these various passages from the last book of the Torah, Moses comes across as an obedient servant, surrendering to God's decree with barely a word of complaint.

Moses' Death in Midrash — The Five Stages of Dying

But something seems amiss in the verses from Torah. Experience working with the dying suggests that, in sometimes uncanny ways, an individual's response to their impending death often mirrors the style of how they lived their life. In Moses' passive, milquetoast reaction to his death decree, we do not see any traces of the courageous leader who challenged the Egyptian slavery system of Pharaoh and his taskmasters, nor the tempestuous lawgiver who, in his hasty rage broke the first set of tablets, and then had the perseverance to return another forty days to Mt. Sinai for a second set of tablets. Given the fiery passion with which Moses lived his life, it seems something is missing in these Torah narratives.

To get a more complete picture of Moses' end-of-life drama, we turn to Midrash and find there an exceptionally elaborate legendary delineation of Moses' death, portraying a radically different point-of-view than the one in Deuteronomy.

In Midrash Deuteronomy Rabbah (XI,10); Midrash Tanhuma (Va'ethanan 6); Sifre on Deuteronomy (Piska 305); and Midrash Petirat Moshe (among other texts) can be found extensive textual material describing Moses' cajoling, manipulative and argumentative disputations with God. From the heated conversations between Moses and God that appear in Midrash, not surprisingly, we discover that Moses did not "go gentle into that good night"; instead, he chose to "rage, rage against the dying of the light"—in the words of the poet Dylan Thomas. Midrash depicts a fascinating range of Moses' reactions to his death, accompanied by passionate self-advocacy for a stay of execution. He believed he was rightfully entitled to enter the Promised Land, and, at least according to Midrash, did all he could to change God's decree, although to no avail.

Midrashim presented below, culled from Deuteronomy Rabbah and Tanhuma, illuminate Moses' process of psychological transformation in response to the imminence of his death. Based upon the work of Rabbi Allan Kensky,[61] we see that Moses goes through, what amounts to, the five stages of dying—denial, anger, bargaining, depression and acceptance—as articulated by the Swiss-born psychiatrist, Dr. Elisabeth Kübler-Ross.[62] Each stage has its own characteristic emotional reactions, leading towards a slow and yet inevitable acceptance of death.

Denial

When first told that he shall not enter the Promised Land, Moses completely sidesteps the import of the decree, rather overtly denying its inevitability. According to Deuteronony Rabbah, after the Heavenly Tribunal decreed his death-sentence, Moses just ignored it, assuming it really did not apply to him. His reasoning was that since God had previously forgiven the people of Israel whenever requested to do so, God would simply do the same on his behalf:

> Israel have many times committed great
> sins, and whenever I prayed for them, God
> immediately answered my prayer, as it is said,
> Let Me alone, that I may destroy them (Deut.
> 9:14); yet what is written there? And the Lord
> repented of the evil (Ex. 32:14) ... Seeing then
> that I have not sinned from my youth, does it
> not stand to reason that when I pray on my
> own behalf God should answer my prayer?
> (Deut. R. XI, 10)

Even knowing that the decree against him had
been sealed, Moses' denial of his death persisted,
and we see him continuing to assume that his
actions would vanquish death's inevitability:

> ... he took a resolve to fast, and drew a small
> circle and stood therein, and exclaimed: "I
> will not move from here until You annul that
> decree." What else did Moses do then? He
> donned sackcloth and wrapped himself with
> sackcloth and rolled himself in the dust and
> stood in prayer and supplications before God,
> until the heavens and the order of nature were
> shaken. (Deut. R. XI, 10)

This attitude of ignoring the echoes of the
inescapable call of death is frequently observed

among people dealing with cancer and other forms of illness. As Kübler-Ross observed: "the need for denial exists in every patient at time, at the very beginning of a serious illness."[63] The truth is, as both Sigmund Freud[64] and Ernst Becker[65] observed, as mortal human beings we have a hard time seeing our own demise. People often need time to accept the inevitability of their own death, and Moses is no exception.

All too often it is easy to respond with judgment or derision when people are frantically seeking every kind of traditional and alternative treatment to what appears to be a terminal diagnosis. But it is important to understand that the need to deny the inevitability of death and fight for one's life is part of the very nature of being human. What is most helpful for those in this situation is to offer loving support and compassion to those—who just like Moses—avoid staring their own death in the face while assiduously denying and defying death's call.

Anger

We know from the experiences of being with people who are dying that their psycho-emotional responses keep changing. With Moses, in passages from Midrash Tanhuma, suddenly we see the headstrong, cantankerous Moses re-emerge.

He is argumentative with God, belligerent, even somewhat sarcastic. In the tone of his dialogue with God, we see Moses' anger about his imminent death:

> "For naught have my feet stepped on the clouds. For naught have I run before you like a horse, as now I will become as a worm" ... God said to him: "I have already decreed death on the first human." Said Moses: "Then let the first human die, for you commanded him one small *mitzvah* and he transgressed it, but don't let me die!" ... God said to him: "But Abraham who sanctified in my name in the world died." Said he: "Abraham begat Ishmael, whose descendants provoke you" ... God said to him: "Isaac who spread his neck on the altar died." Said Moses to God: "Isaac who begat Esau who destroyed the Temple and burnt your sanctuary." God said: "Look at Jacob who begat twelve tribes of whom none were unfit." Said he to God: "Jacob did not go up to heaven; neither did he step on the clouds, nor was he like the ministering angels. You did not speak to him face to face and he didn't receive the Torah from you." (Tanhuma, V'Ethchanan 6).

Here Moses is comparing himself with others who have come before him, reminding God of how loyal a servant he has been. Adam, he says, was asked to do one *mitzvah*—not eat from the Tree of Knowledge—and he disobeyed! Abraham brought Ishmael into the world "whose descendants provoke you" (understood in the context of the time to mean Muslims); Isaac brought Esau into the world, whose descendants destroyed the Temple; none of Jacob's descendants were righteous. But I Moses—he claims—spoke to you God face to face and received your Torah. Angrily reciting his resume of accomplishments to God, here is vociferously advocating for himself and rationalizing why he should not die.

But all Moses' emotionality not withstanding, God held steadfast in His decree. The text informs us that God bolted the gates of heaven to ensure Moses' prayers would not be accepted, and that he not be granted continued life, nor enter the Holy Land. (Ibid)

So in spite of Moses' angry protestations, nothing changed! Similarly, in the context of caring for the dying, we often see people facing death getting angry at doctors and other medical personnel, at family, at the small little upsets of life. The anger is a frustrated response to the powerlessness in the face of illness and dying. While uncomfortable for family and care-givers, anger is one of the many predictable stages in the process of wrestling with a decree of death.

Bargaining

Seeing that neither denial nor anger were effective, Moses became more desperate, and began bargaining with God:

"Master of the Universe," said Moses, "if You will not bring me into the Land of Israel, leave me in this world so that I may live and not die." (Deut. R. XI, 10) [God's refusal was swift. Again Moses pleaded:] "Master of the Universe, if You will not bring me into the Land of Israel, let me become like the beasts of the field that eat grass and drink water and live and enjoy the world; likewise let my soul be as one of them." (Ibid.) [God was unrelenting, but so was Moses:] "Master of the Universe, if not, let me become in this world like the bird that flies about in every direction, and gathers its food daily, and returns to its nest towards evening; let my soul likewise become like one of them." (Ibid.)

All the machinations of Moses' bargaining were ineffective, and did nothing to alter his fate. God was unmoved and once again silenced Moses. Being unrelenting, Moses continued his pleading in various ways, begging for mercy of heaven, earth, sun, moon, stars, planets, mountains,

73

hills, and ocean; sadly none of those forces of the universe were able to intervene on Moses' behalf. In these grasping and desperate final acts, we see how willing Moses is to go to all ends of the earth to stay alive and to experience the unfulfilled vision of his life, to enter the Promised Land.

This is very similar to what we see how dying people are more than willing to subject themselves to all kinds of medical treatments and procedures with the hope of staying alive, while knowing at some level their demise is inevitable. Just like we see with Moses' bargaining, the desperate pleading and bargaining leads nowhere, only to a slowly dawning awareness that the inevitable end is approaching.

Depression

Continuing his manipulative machinations, eventually Moses appeals to a transcendental, supernal being known as *Sar Panim* (Minister of the Interior), one of many angelic presences in Rabbinic literature. But even here, Moses' words fell on deaf ears. "Moses, my master, why all this trouble?" the angel responds with dispassionate veracity: "I have already heard from behind the curtain that your prayer will not listened to in this matter." (Tanhuma, V'Ethchanan 6) Sorry Moses, he is told, looks like you are running out of options.

In this retort, the reality of his impending death came home to Moses with powerful impact: "Moses put his hands on his head, and cried, who will pray for me?" (Ibid.) It is clear at this point that the stage of depression has set in. Like a cancer patient who has just been told there are no more treatment options, Moses is finally beginning to see the inevitable. Death is staring him in the face, and it hurts. For the very first time there are genuine tears of grief. Moses' personal identity is beginning to dissolve, no longer is he the invincible leader who talked with Pharaoh and split the sea; climbed mountains and inspired an unruly nation for forty years. Vulnerable and defenseless, Moses confesses to God: "I am afraid of the angel of death." (Ibid.)

Even as his defenses begin to wear down, Moses is not yet ready to surrender to his own demise. As one close to death, he desperately needs comfort from those around him. With his brother and sister already dead, Moses, the man of the mountain, yearns for tender comfort from the God who has been his life-long ally and nemesis. He begs: "Do not hand me over into the hand of the Angel of Death." (Deut. R. XI, 10) In response to his fear, *Bat Kol*, a divine emissary—an aspect of the transcendent God that manifests in the human realm—comforts Moses: "Fear not, I myself will attend to you and your burial." (Ibid.)

We see in these texts an exact mirroring of what

goes on for people in staring their own death right in the face. After the emotional roller coaster of denial of death, angry outbursts against God and manipulative machinations to try and change his destined decree, Moses realizes that his death cannot be stayed. He falls into a depressed sense of despair. But at the same time, we see him honor and accept his vulnerability. And it is this exact process that is evidenced so frequently when people realize there are no more medical treatments which can give them any sense of hope that they might live. There are no more maybes, there is only the reality and inevitability of death. Then, as we see with Moses, the only and best option is to open up to being with surrounding family and friends, and with God, in a spirit of humble vulnerability.

Acceptance

In the interplay of parallel, but variant, texts in Tanhuma and Deuteronomy Rabbah, we see Moses' life wind down, as he moves towards an acceptance of his death, and a peaceful resolution with God and with the Israelite nation. Tanhuma describes how Moses sees Joshua taking over as teacher of the Israelite nation. Seeing this Moses seems to relax knowing his legacy shall continue and he is finally able surrender to God: "Master of the Universe, until now I have asked for life, now my life is given to you." (Tanhuma, v'Etchanan 6)

As the struggle dissipates, and Moses finally begins to accept the reality of his death, an odd shift transpires. We see here that the polarity of conflict between God and Moses breaks down: with Moses no longer fighting desperately to stay alive and defy his ordained fate, God too begins to grieve, lamenting the loss of his long-time champion and defender.

> Once Moses accepted his death, God opened and said: "Who will take my part against evil men?" (Ps. 94:16). Who will stand up for Israel in the time of my anger, who will fight the battles of my children, who will seek mercy for them when they sin before me? (Tanhuma, v'Etchanan 6)

Reflecting the human dynamic in acceptance of one's own death, in Midrash Tanhuma we see how Moses now focuses on the completion of his relationship with the Israelite people. Satisfied that his legacy will continue through Joshua, Moses can reach far beyond his individual suffering and gives his final blessings to the nation, as recorded in Deuteronomy—"This is the blessing, with which Moses the man of God blessed the people of Israel before his death." (Deut. 33:1) Moses asks for forgiveness for the pain he caused the people in bringing them the Torah and the *mitzvot*. In turn, Israel asks Moses for forgiveness for the pain they have caused their revered leader. Closure takes place, all is forgiven, and after an exhausting ordeal Moses is finally and unequivocally prepared to die.

The moment of death arrives, and after all the *Sturm und Drang*, God and Moses are no longer in an adversarial relationship with one another. The final moments are full of blessing. Moses experiences the most peaceful death possible, the kiss of God:

> At that hour, Moses arose and sanctified himself like the Seraphim, and God came down from the highest heavens to take away the soul of Moses, and with Him were three ministering angels, Michael, Gabriel, and Zagzagel. Michael laid out his bier, Gabriel spread out a fine linen cloth at his bolster, Zagzagel one at his feet; Michael stood at one side and Gabriel at the other side. God said: "Moses, fold your eyelids over your eyes," and he did so. He then said: "Place your hands upon your breast," and he did so. He then said: "Put your feet next to one another," and he did so. Forthwith the Holy One, blessed be He, summoned the soul from the midst of the body, saying to her: "My daughter, I have fixed the period of your stay in the body of Moses

at a hundred and twenty years; now your end has come, depart, delay not ... Thereupon God kissed Moses and took away his soul with a kiss of the mouth ... (Deut. R. XI, 10)

Finally, as the grand finale to a sacred story of wandering and yearning to live the destiny of God's calling, the Torah so eloquently and simply reminds us:

There never was another prophet in Israel like Moses, whom God knew face to face. No one else could have performed all the wonders and miracles that God allowed Moses to perform before Pharaoh, in the land of Egypt, or any of the powerful miracles and awesome deeds that Moses performed before the eyes of all the Israelites. (Deut. 34:10-11)

From this creative collage of *midrashim,* we see a far more elaborate depiction of Moses' death than that delineated in Torah. In the multifaceted range of emotions experienced by Moses, we see the essential nature of the human encounter with death—stark and unadorned, passionate and dramatic but full of potential for healing and redemption. What Moses went through in his intense pleading for life, mirrors the kind of processes family members and friends go through in dealing with terminal illness and end-of-life dramas. What we learn from Moses, in both life and in death, is to live with authenticity, following one's destiny, wrestling with God and striving for a life imbued with a sense of God's presence. It is this above all which will guide us dealing with the ultimate end-of-life callings all human beings are destined to experience.

Envisioning a Renewed
Philosophy of Death

*Transforming Cultural Attitudes
Towards Death and Dying*

There is a multi-textured richness found in both Torah and Midrash with regard to Jewish notions of death, dying, burial and mourning. While undoubtedly more can be written on these topics, what emerges from this study is an appreciation of the richness Jewish tradition offers for exploring all facets of the human encounter with death. The final question to be addressed here is—what are the contemporary implications of these various ideas of death, burial and mourning found in Biblical and Rabbinic tradition?

To put this discussion in context: in 1900, Sigmund Freud published *The Interpretation of Dreams* outlining his psychoanalytical, psycho-sexual theories. Intentionally published as the new century was beginning, this seminal work inaugurated an ongoing process of transformation of cultural attitudes towards sexuality. One hundred and fifteen years later, this process is still unfolding; and while much has changed, there is still a long way to go as we endeavor to find right approaches to human sexuality and gender dynamics in our culture.

In 1969, Elisabeth Kübler-Ross published *On Death and Dying*, a book that inaugurated a profound process of cultural transformation of attitudes towards dying and death. In the less than half-century since the publication of Kübler-Ross' first book, a revolution in attitudes towards the dying and bereaved has unfolded in many different ways.

Through the development of hospice, there has been a proliferation compassionate approaches toward caring for the dying. While controversial, there is an emerging openness to physician-assisted death for those who suffer interminably. There are new developments in burial and funeral care, with a return to simple burial, "do-it-yourself" funerals, and a growing interest in "green burial." In the area of bereavement, there is a wide spectrum of resources available for those in mourning. At the same time, over the decades, a deeper understanding of the nature and implications of near-death experiences has entered the culture, changing ways we think about the experience of death and the afterdeath experience. Similarly, esoteric and spiritual approaches to dying and death have come from other cultures such as

Tibetan and Zen Buddhism, and are slowly being infused into Western death care practices. And over all, a spiritual view of the human encounter with death is slowly but surely being integrated into our culture.

Clearly, in the wake of Kübler-Ross' pioneering work, there is an ongoing transformation of cultural responses to death and this will certainly continue in the coming years and decades. Against this background, what is the wisdom and understanding that Biblical tradition offers to further catalyze and transform attitudes towards dying and death? What can we extract from our study of motifs of death and mourning in Biblical tradition to inform the contemporary revolution in death care?

An Attitude of Openness Toward Death

First of all, in the deathbed stories of our Biblical ancestors, we see an attitude of honesty and openness towards death. Abraham is not anxious and fear-filled when having to purchase a burial chamber for his wife Sarah. Neither Jacob nor Joseph are in denial of their inevitable death, but instead speak openly and comfortably with their families about their impending demise. These stories provide us with an ideal model for learning to deal more openly with death and dying in our families, to be able to speak honestly with spouses, children and siblings about our own and each other's death and final wishes. The ideal we want to strive for is to create a culture that is not "deathophobic," but one that is more open and honest with regard to the reality of death. We can learn this from the ways in which our Biblical ancestors responded to death.

Death is a Transition

Another aspect of the revolution in death care is that we are slowly but surely moving away from a materialistic model of the human being, and beginning to recognize that death itself is not finite, and that there is a consciousness that survives bodily death. The rationalistic, materialistic model asserts that death is the end: it is if as one pulls the plug, the brain goes dead, and dead is dead. Period. But in Biblical tradition, specifically in the death of Rachel, we read how Rachel's soul seemed to ebb away gently: *b'tzait naphsha*—"as her soul was departing"—are the words found in Genesis 37:18. In Biblical tradition, death is regarded as a process of the soul gently and gradually leaving behind the physical body. It is this awareness that we want to infuse and integrate more fully into our medical and hospice care for the dying. If it is not a violent accidental death or a sudden cardiac arrest, people do die slowly, and the soul gradually dissipates from the body. To recognize that as a fact of death care has profound implications for how we respond to the needs of the dying and their families. We are still in the early phases of creating a spiritually-based model of dying and death, and it is clear we can learn something from the spiritual wisdom inherent in the Biblical view of dying and death.

Understanding the Ever-Changing Needs of the Dying

In the legendary depictions of Moses' death in Midrash, we see the process that Kübler-Ross describes taking place for those dealing with terminal illness. Above all, we see how important it is to have a patient and compassionate understanding of what is happening with the dying. Moses himself, the spiritual leader of the Hebrew nation, had such a hard time accepting his own death; how much more difficult is dying for younger fathers and mothers, or elders who may not have "crossed into the Promised Land" and fulfilled the dreams of their lives. From the Moses material, we are reminded to be continually empathic and caring for the dying. We want to create a culture that accepts death as part of life and brings the compassion of a caring heart to those who are traversing through the end-of-life journey.

In Dying There is a Connection with Previous Generations

Upon their death, it is said that Abraham, Isaac, Jacob and Moses are each "gathered to his people." In a similar motif, both King Solomon and King David "slept with his ancestors." The understanding of these terms in the ancient world is that they are literal not figurative metaphors. As we have seen, death for our Biblical ancestors was very specifically understood as a return to the postmortem realm of the dead and a re-connection with deceased ancestors. This notion of a reunion with deceased loved ones is documented over and over in studies of near-death experiences. And dying persons frequently report seeing loved ones at the bedside. We want to envision an approach to death and dying in which this is not a random interesting thought or factoid, but is in fact part of our normative understanding of death and the experience. In death, one re-connects with loved ones. Recent studies of the "deathing"[66] experience suggests that this is the case, and if death is a transition, one aspect of this transition is to be gathered to the realm of the ancestors. This idea has important pastoral implications in how we care for the dying and help people accept the reality of death. For many, there can be comfort in knowing that one's deceased loved ones will be there to greet and welcome a person in their dying.

There is Great Variability in Death and Bereavement Rituals

As a more open attitude toward death and dying spreads, people are generally more willing to practice traditional death and mourning rituals, and also to experiment with newer rituals and practices. In exploring Biblical mourning practices, we observed a wide diversity of options and traditions. The point to be made here is that Jewish death, burial and mourning rituals have evolved over millennia and have always had a wide diversity of styles and practices. Yes, there may be specific specific halakhic, legalistic guidelines for practice. But at the same time, over the course of history there has always been a great variability of cultural styles of mourning and specific ritual practices. This study of Biblical tradition provides inspiration to explore and experiment with new Jewish death rituals, particularly as noted earlier, with bringing contemplative flute music and wailing traditions back into contemporary funeral practice.

Judaism has a Long-Standing Legacy of Death Practices

And finally, to conclude this study, it is important to realize that so many of today's Jewish death practices have roots in ancient Biblical customs that date back over three (and perhaps four) millennia. The traditions which Judaism offers are rich, multi-layered and above all can be functional and efficacious in people's lives. This study of motifs of death, burial and mourning in the Hebrew Bible teaches us, above all, that Jewish death traditions have both a long history and at the same time an unwritten and exciting future.

Notes and References

1 Elizabeth Kübler-Ross, *On Death and Dying* (New York: Macmillan Publishing Company, 1969).

2 Rachel S. Hallote, *Death, Burial, and Afterlife in the Biblical World* (Chicago: Ivan R. Dee, 2001).

3 Philip S. Johnston, *Shades of Sheol: Death and Afterlife in the Old Testament* (Downers Grove, Ill: InterVarsity Press, 2002).

4 Saul M. Olyan, *Biblical Mourning: Ritual and Social Dimensions* (New York: Oxford University Press, 2004).

5 Xuan Huong Thi Pham, *Mourning in the Ancient Near East and the Hebrew Bible* (Sheffield, England: Sheffield Academic Press, 1999).

6 Nicholas J. Tromp, *Primitive Conceptions of Death and Afterlife the Nether World in the Old Testament* (Rome: Pontifical Biblical Institute, 1969).

7 The work of Chinitz was helpful in this task: Jacob Chinitz, "Death in the Bible" *Jewish Bible Quarterly*, 32,2 (Apr-Jun 2004) 98-103.

8 See John W. Cooper, *Body, Soul and Everlasting Life—Biblical Anthropology and the Monism-Dualism Debate* (Grand Rapids, MI: William B. Eerdmans Publishing Co, 1989).

9 See Elizabeth Bloch-Smith, *Judahite Burial Practices and Beliefs about the Dead* (Sheffield, England: Sheffield Academic Press, 1992; Herbert Chanan Brichto, "Kin, Cult, Land and Afterlife—A Biblical Complex," *Hebrew Union College Annual* 44 (1973), p. 8; Hallote, pp. 61-68.

In the early Talmudic period, it was common for families to place the bones of the deceased into carved ossuaries; this took place about one year after a death. (See Moses Maimonides, *Mishneh Torah,* Sefer Shoftim, Evel, 12:8) See also Steven Fine, "A Note on Ossuary Burial and the Resurrection of the Dead in First Century Jerusalem," *Journal of Jewish Studies* 51 (2000), pp. 67–76.

10 An alternate translation here could be "mummified him".

11 Chinitz, p. 100.

12 Ibid.

13 Raymond Moody, *Life After Life* (New York: Bantam Books, 1976); Michael Sabom, *Recollections of Death—A Medical Investigation* (New York: Simon and Shuster, 1982).

14 See Peter Fenwick and Elizabeth Fenwick, *The Art of Dying* (New York: Continuum Books, 2008) in which the authors describe frequent visions of deceased relatives in deathbed visions—what they refer to as "end-of-life experiences" (ELEs).

15 Chinitz, pp. 100-101.

16 Shaul Bar, *I Deal Death and Give Life—Biblical*

Perspectives on Death (Piscatawy, NJ: Gorgias Press LLC, 2010) pp. 305-306.

17 Ibid.

18 In Rabbinic literature, Machpelah takes on a mythic quality, with Midrash claiming that not only the Patriarchs and Matriarchs but also Adam and Eve are buried at Machpelah. (Gen. R. 53:4)

19 Ibid, p. 304. See also Raphael Patai, *Sex and Family in Bible and the Middle East* (Garden City, N.Y.: Doubleday and Co., 1959) pp. 233ff.

20 Walter Eichrodt, *Theology of the Old Testament, Vol. II.* trans. J.A. Baker (London: SCM Press, 1967), pp. 213ff. R.H. Charles, *Eschatology—The Doctrine of a Future Life in Israel, Judaism and Christianity* (New York: Schocken Books, 1963), p. 32. Patai, Ibid.

21 The foregoing is based upon Simcha Paull Raphael, *Jewish Views of the Afterlife, second edition* (Lanham, MD: Rowman and Littlefield, 2009) pp. 43-46.

22 Brichto, p. 8.

23 The notion of a pillar as a memorial monument in ancient times may be inaccurate. More likely, it was a pile of stones that was placed over the grave of Rachel.

24 Denys Pringle, *The Churches of the Crusader Kingdom of Jerusalem: L-Z* (Cambridge: Cambridge University Press, 1998, p. 176) cited in "Rachel's Tomb", *Wikipedia: The Free Encyclopedia;* (Wikimedia Foundation Inc.);

available from http://en.wikipedia.org/wiki/ Rachel's Tomb

25 The term used here, *la'ḥanot,* is usually translated as "to embalm." However, I have chosen to use the word "mummify" and "mummification" through this book, in place of "embalming."

Today the word embalming has a very different connotation than it would have had in ancient Egypt. In ancient times, what is called embalming —*la'ḥanot*—was likely a process of annointing a body with oil and spices. Today, however, embalming is a process of draining blood and injecting a preservative to make the body appear life-like. That was not what was practiced in ancient Egyptian culture. In Egypt, the mummification process consisted of removing internal organs, rinsing out and drying the body, and after seventy days wrapping the body with from head to toe in bandages and placing the body in a sarcophagus, a type of box like a coffin. It seems that this is what is being referred to in the Genesis text.

My thanks to David Zinner, of Kavod v'Nichum, for these observations.

26 A.J. Spencer, *Death in Ancient Egypt* (New York: Penguin Books, 1983). See also Herodotus, II, 84-88 in which he describes three different types of embalmment. My thanks to Dr. Jean Ouellette for this reference.

27 Archaeological evidence indicates that the dead

were laid to rest on rock shelves within family burial caves, and later the bones may have been gathered and placed in a collective depository. See Eichrodt, *Theology of the Old Testament, Vol. II.* pp. 213ff.; Eric Meyers, *Jewish Ossuaries: Reburial and Rebirth* (Rome: Biblical Institute Press, 1971).

28 Hallote, p. 117ff.

29 Spencer, pp, 112ff.

30 Ibid, p. 120.

31 Schubert Spero, "The Funeral of Jacob: A Joint Hebrew-Egyptian Affair," *Jewish Bible Quarterly*, 26,1 (Jan-Mar 1998) p. 20.

32 Ibid.

33 Spero suggests that in this period of history, the Hyksos rather than the Egyptian ruled the hill country of Canaan and the lower Negev, requiring an Egyptian travel party to take a longer route to Hebron. Ibid, p. 23-24.

34 See Numbers, Ch. 2.

35 Ibid, p. 24.

36 Spencer, pp. 51-52.

37 Ibid, p. 52.

38 See John F. Sawyer, "Hebrew Words for the Resurrection of the Dead," *Vetus Testamentum*, XXIII, (1973), 218-234.

39 See Raphael, pp. 68-74; 156-160.

40 Jean Houston, *The Passion of Isis and Osiris: A Gateway to Transcendent Love* (New York:

Random House, 1995).

41 Tamara Cohn Eskenazi and Andrea L. Weiss (eds.), *The Torah: A Women's Commentary* (New York: URJ Press, 2008) p. 383.

42 Olyan, pp. 30-31.

43 Francis Brown, S.R. Driver and C.A. Briggs. *Hebrew and English Lexicon of the Old Testament.* (Oxford: Clarendon Press, 1907; 1968), p. 704.

44 Bar 317-318.

45 Olyan, p 31, ft.nt. 11.

46 Olyan, p. 35.

47 Ibid.

48 Dayan H. Lazarus (trans.), *Hebrew-English Edition of the Babylonian Talmud - Moed Katan* (London: The Soncino Press, 1990); and Dov Zlotnick, (trans. and ed.), *The Tractate 'Mourning' - (Semahot).* (New Haven: Yale University Press, 1966.

49 Morris Jastrow, "Dust, Earth and Ashes as Symbols of Mourning Among the Ancient Hebrews" *Journal of the American Oriental Society,* Vol. XX (1899) 133-150.

50 Olyan, p. 29.

51 Bar, p. 333. See also MK 27b, Sem. 9:2.

52 See Chaim Denberg (ed.), *Code of Hebrew Law— Shulhan 'Aruk, Yoreh Deah 335-403* (Montreal: Jurisprudence Press, 1954).

53 At the time of sitting *Shiva* for both my parents, each time I chose to don a black vest, which was

ripped symbolically and which I wore throughout week of mourning.

54 See "Poems About Baal Anat," (trans. H.L. Ginsberg), in James B. Pritchard, *Ancient Near Eastern Texts Relating to the Old Testament* (Princeton, NJ: Princeton University Press, 1969) p. 125, quoted by Bar p. 340.

55 Bar, Ibid.

56 See Gary Anderson, *A Time to Mourn, A Time to Dance—Expression of Grief and Joy in Israelite Religion* (University Park, PA: Pennsylvania State University Press, 1991).

57 While *kinah* and its plural *kinot* are the terms used to describe funerary dirges in the Hebrew Bible, Amos 5:16 has an infrequently used term *nehi* to speak of songs of lamentation.

58 Bar, p. 313.

59 Ibid, p. 50.

60 Bar, p. 313. See Jennifer Joy Goldstein Lewis, *The Meqonenot and Beyond: Female Voices in Communal Prayer, Rabbinic Thesis, New York: Hebrew Union College—Jewish Institute of Religion* (March 2005), and Tova Gamliel, *Aesthetics of Sorrow—The Wailing Culture of Yemenite Jewish Women*, trans. Tova Gamliel (Detroit: Wayne State University, 2014).

61 Allan Kensky, "On Death and Dying and the Last Days of Moses," *Reconstructionist* (Spring 1992), 25-27.

62 Kübler-Ross.

63 Ibid, p. 41.

64 Sigmund Freud, "Thoughts for the Times on War and Death," *Standard Edition of the Complete Psychological Works of Sigmund Freud,* trans. and ed. James Strachey (London: Hogarth Press, 1953-1974) 14:273-302, 1915.

65 Ernst Becker, *The Denial of Death* (New York: The Free Press, 1973).

66 This term is used by Kathleen Dowling Singh, *The Grace in Dying* (San Francisco: Harper San Francisco, 1998).

DA'AT INSTITUTE

DEATH AWARENESS, ADVOCACY *and* TRAINING

THE DA'AT INSTITUTE is dedicated to providing death awareness education and professional development training. Working in consultation with synagogues, churches, hospice programs and other types of community organizations, THE Da'at Institute offers:

1. *Educational Programs* on death, dying, bereavement, and the spirituality of end-of-life issues and concerns.

2. *Professional Development Training* to clergy, health care and mental health professionals and educators working with the dying and bereaved.

3. *Bereavement and Hospice Counseling Services* to individuals and families through counseling, professional referral and bereavement support groups.

4. *Rituals of Transition* for dying, burial, bereavement, unveiling and memorialization, helping families create meaningful rituals of passage.

5. *Printed and Audio-Visual Resources* on the various facets of dealing with grief and loss, and on the spirituality of death and afterlife.

The Da'at Institute
1211 Ansley Avenue
Melrose Park, PA 19027
drsimcha@daatinstitute.net
www.daatinstitute.net

REB SIMCHA PAULL RAPHAEL, Ph.D. is Founding Director of the DA'AT Institute for Death Awareness, Advocacy and Training (www.daatinstitute.net). He received his doctorate in Psychology from the California Institute of Integral Studies and was ordained as a Rabbinic Pastor by Rabbi Zalman Schachter-Shalomi. He is Adjunct Professor in Religion at Temple University and LaSalle University, works as a psychotherapist and spiritual director in Philadelphia and is a Fellow of the Rabbis Without Borders Network. He has written extensively on death and afterlife and is author of the groundbreaking *Jewish Views of the Afterlife.*

Made in the USA
Coppell, TX
28 March 2024

30665109R00069